FUZZBEAN CROSSING

Heartfelt Remembrances of Ferrets That
Have Crossed the Rainbow Bridge

By Donna G. Austin
Illustrated by Marta C. Mitchell

Copyright © 2002 Donna G. Austin

All rights reserved. No part of this publication may be reproduced, stored in a retrieval system or transmitted in any form or by any means electronic, mechanical, photocopying, recording or otherwise, without the prior written permission of the publisher.

Published by Pogo Publishing
9493 Dutch Hollow Road
Rixeyville, VA 22737
540-937-7953

Cover illustration by Marta C. Mitchell

ISBN 0-9723521-0-4

THE DANCE
Words and Music by TONY ARATA
© 1989 MORGANACTIVE SONGS, INC. and EMI APRIL MUSIC INC.
All Rights on behalf of EMI APRIL MUSIC INC.
Administered by MORGAN MUSIC GROUP INC.
All Rights on behalf of MORGANACTIVE SONGS, INC.
and EMI APRIL MUSIC INC. outside the United States and Canada
Administered by WB MUSIC CORP.
All Rights Reserved Used by Permission
Warner Bros. Publications U.S. Inc., Miami, Florida 33014

THE NEW RAINBOW BRIDGE
© 1998 Steve and Diane Bodofsky
389 Clair Road
Southampton, PA 18966
215-357-6071/800-259-1745
All Rights Reserved Used by Permission

All stories contained herein are used by permission of the authors.

Disclaimer: The health and safety tips throughout the book are observations and lessons learned through personal experience living with ferrets. I am not a medical professional and the content of the following pages is not meant to replace medical advice given by an experienced ferret veterinarian.   - Donna Austin

Printed in the United States by Morris Publishing
3212 East Highway 30
Kearney, NE 68847
1-800-650-7888

FUZZBEAN CROSSING

DEDICATION

To my children Kelly and Troy who have never understood my affection for ferrets, and Aron, the son who brought ferrets into my life and started me on my ferret adventure over 10 years ago. To my first two ferrets, Demi Sioux and Warlock, I'll always remember how special you were and how you taught me to be happy with the *little* things in life. You all changed my life forever.

TABLE OF CONTENTS

Acknowledgments xiii
Introduction xv
In Memoriam xviii
Rainbow Bridge 2

A

Aislyn, Alexander, Almond 3-8

B

Baby, Bailey George, Bandit (3), Barnaby, Barret, Beans, Bear (2), Betty, Bo, Bones (2), Booger, BreAnna Lynn, Bubby, Buckwheat, Buddy (2), Buttercup 9-35

C

Cael, Caesar, Callie, Cassidy Sioux, Chandler, Cherokee, Chicky, Chomper, Chuck, Chuckie, Clydesdale, Colonel Sanders, Custard 36-50

D

Dakota TBear, Dementia Sioux, Diana and Epimetheus 51-54

E

Eloise, Ethan 55-58

F

Fatboy Slim, Fresno, Furry, Fuzzy 59-62

G

Godiva, Gonzo, Gypsy 63-65

H

Handsome, Heidi, Hermes, Houdini, Hubert, Humphrey 66-72

J

JB, Jasmine (3), Jasper (2), Jeremy, Jesse, Jewel, Junior 73-87

K

Kari, Kasper, Katie, Kirby, Koala, Kuma, Kyle 88-95

L

Little Fang, Littleone, Love, Lucky (2) 96-104

M

Major Burns, Mandrake, Maxie, Maximilian, Meep, Miss Kitty, Mistie Sioux, Mocha, Monkey, Mr. Edward, Mr. Noble Man, Mr. Peabody, Murray 105-122

N

Nipper 123

O

Odie, Oldguy, Opie 124-126

P

PB, Paladin, Pato, Peanut, Peedee, PePe,
Pjatten, Pogo, Popcorn, Pugsley 127-138

Q

Quasimoto 139

R

Rascal, Rebecca Sioux, Renate, Renny,
Rocky (2), Romeo, Rusty (2) 141-152

S

Sammy, Samson, Sandie, Sassy, Simba, Skyler,
Snowy, Sonny (2), Sophie, Squeeky and Snowball,
Stevie, Stinky, Surabi, Sweet Amadeus Van Gogh,
Sweetie 153-173

T

Tasha (2), Tassie, Tawnee Sioux, Thelma,
Tia, Tiny, Tootles, Tucker (2), Tyson 176-190

W

Wanda, Warlock, Whiskey Sour, White Russian (2),
Winnie, Wolf 191-200

Z

Zeus (2), Ziggy (2), Zorro, Zuzu 201-206

APPENDIX

DEALING WITH GRIEF 211
BOOKS ON GRIEF 214
COMMON MEDICAL CONDITIONS IN FERRETS 216
    Adrenal Disease 216
    Aleutian's Disease (ADV) 217
    Anemia 217
    Dental Conditions 218
    Epizootic Catarrhal Enteritis (ECE) 218
    Enlarged Lymph Nodes 219
    Hairball or Foreign Body 219
    Insulinoma 220
    Intestinal or Liver Abnormalities 220
    Prolapsed Rectum 221
    Spleen Tumors 222
MEDICATIONS USED FOR TREATING FERRETS 223
THE ACUPUNCTURE TREATMENT AS TOLD BY JAKOB ... 225
PLANTS TOXIC TO PETS 227

HELPFUL CHARTS
Nail Clipping and Ear Cleaning Chart 231
Weight Chart 232
Medication Chart 234

INSTRUCTIONS & PATTERNS
Creating a Ferret Room 239
How to Make Fleece "Double Stuff" Ferret Hammocks 244
How to Make Cozy Ferret Sleeping Bags 246

WONDERFUL WEBSITES TO VISIT 248
Grief 248
Medical Information and Facilities 248
Memorial Gardens 249
Miscellaneous 250
Remembrance Products 252
Urns and Markers 252

Index 253

ILLUSTRATION LIST

Ferret Angel	xix
Albino and Sable Friends	28
I'm So Sleepy	56
Let Me Out Please	84
Mischievous One in Planter Pot	118
Babies and Bunnies	144
It's So Tasty	174
Ferret on a Cloud	207

POETRY LIST

The Visit	xx
The Rainbow Bridge	29
A Fuzzy's Prayer	57
Blessings	85
Whispers	119
Little One	145
A Tidy House	175
The Dance	208

ACKKNOWLEDGMENTS

Thank you Dr. Charlie Weiss, for not only reviewing the book, but showing such compassion, kindness and expertise while treating my ferrets over the years. You have mended so many of them and, if it weren't for you, they would not be here with me today.

To Dr. Sonja Olson, thank you for taking time while on vacation to read the manuscript for medical accuracy. I would also like to say, "Welcome to our family."

Thank you to editor Jason Konopinski, for the willingness to put himself through such an emotional experience. Undoubtedly, he learned a lot about ferrets in the process.

To Caitie Bergeron, one of us "ferret" people, who read the book and, through her tears, gave me helpful feedback on it and shared her ferret stories with me. Thank you from the bottom of my heart.

And, of course, to the ferret lovers everywhere who wrote such beautiful and heartfelt stories about their beloved pets; thank you all for letting me share your stories with so many others. If it weren't for you, there wouldn't be a book at all.

INTRODUCTION

In the summer of 1992, two tiny white ferrets came into my life and managed to creep silently into my heart. From that time on, I would never look at life the same again. Through the years I have brought into my home young ferrets, not so young ferrets, unloved, abandoned, wandering and neglected ferrets, crippled and abused ferrets. Each one of these special gifts has made me laugh more, cry more, give more and be more. I knew immediately those many years ago what my life's mission was—to take care of homeless ferrets. At the time I wasn't looking for the meaning of life, let alone what to do with the life I had. I was content in my day-to-day existence living with two very independent cats. Ferrets quickly became my all-consuming passion and I began to live and breathe ferrets. I started designing and making unique handcrafted ferret items and began selling them at ferret shows and on the Internet.[1] One year later, in September 1993, I lost one of the first two ferrets and I began to understand how powerful grief really was.

I have always thought "ferret" people were unique and feel differently about their ferrets than "dog" or "cat" people feel about their respective pets, even when it comes to loss. I've talked to a lot of ferret people and read much e-mail that makes me believe this is true. After reading so many stories written to the Ferret Mailing List[2] on the Internet about ferrets that have crossed over the Rainbow Bridge,[3] I decided to publish this collection of letters that touched my heart the most. Each story made me laugh or made me cry. If you are a "dog" or "cat" person, please don't put this book down, keep reading. You will find compassion, comfort and understanding in these stories, especially if you've experienced the loss of a family pet. In addition to my own personal stories of departed ferrets, over 130 others have also been included here. On most of the pages you will also find health and safety tips I've

---

[1] www.ferretsandfriends.com
[2] To subscribe to this list, find the address in the appendix.
[3] See The Rainbow Bridge poem on page 29.

learned by caring for my own ferrets. In the appendix you will find medical information about ferret diseases, helpful charts to help you care for your own ferrets, instructions for setting up a ferret room, making ferret sleeping bags and hammocks as well as related websites to visit.

As I was choosing the stories for this collection, I read each poignant one with great difficulty because so much emotion and deep sadness fills the writing. These stories were written to commemorate not only a death of a much-loved family member, but to celebrate the joyous life of a very special friend. Many tears have fallen onto keyboards all over the world as each story was written. I feel I have come to know each ferret and their human caretakers through these stories and feel the love that fills each household.

This is a collection of love stories more than anything else. Whether you now live with ferrets or are thinking about doing so, I hope you are touched by the stories written by people who, like me, have been smitten by the love of ferrets.

Because I have lost eighteen of my own "furry kids," I can sympathize with anyone who has experienced it. My heart has been broken too many times and it has been the most difficult thing I've ever had to go through. I'm not sure if there is a limit on how many heartbreaks one person can have before the heart is no longer repairable. I do wonder, though, each time I lose another ferret to old age or disease, "Will this be the one from which I can no longer pull myself together and go on?" So far, I've managed to find the strength to take care of just one more ferret. This is what has healed my heart.

Writing about living has also helped me get through the grieving by remembering the joyful day-to-day experiences I've had with my ferrets. When each dies, I make a burial box and fill it with much love and favorite toys. With tears streaming down my face, too many shovelfuls of dirt have painfully been scooped from the earth to make burial plots. All my furry angels are in the backyard, surrounded by the woods behind the house. Two stone garden angels sit at the cemetery's edge, watching over those within its boundaries. Beneath the tall trees surrounding the small cemetery there is a park bench where I can sit and reflect, remembering the happy times and say "hello" once again to my "furry kids." From inside the house the cemetery can also be seen, and it gives me comfort to know they are near. I remember with great fondness all of them and what made each so special.

Don't try to read this book all the way through in one sitting because it will be difficult to do. Read a few stories and then go spend time with your ferrets or other furry family members. I have not included graphic descriptions of sick, hurt or ailing ferrets here in this collection. Although many of you have experienced first-hand the pain, and sometimes the hopelessness, of caring for an ill or hurt ferret, you won't read about it here.

If you ask me if I would trade my totally exhausting, hectic, no-social-life life with ferrets for a more leisurely one of relaxation, a movie or even an occasional date, my immediate reply would be, "No!" Incidentally, the last movie I saw was in 1993 and the last date was around the same time period. I guess that says something about my life or, as "non-ferret" people would think, lack of it. My life would certainly be empty without ferrets in it. Each and every day living with these beautiful creatures brings joy and an occasional sadness, but I'm living my passion and that's the way everyone's life should be.

> Hugs and ferret kisses to fuzzies everywhere,
> Donna
> FuzzbeanCrossing@aol.com

IN MEMORIAM

Dementia "Demi" Sioux
1989-1993

Chuckie "Chuck"
1990-1999

Dakota "Koti" TBear
1993-1996

Cassidy "Cassie" Sioux
1992-1999

Warlock
1990-1996

Sandie
1992-1999

Monkey
1993-1997

Clydesdale "Cubby"
1995-2000

Barnaby "Barn"
1991-1997

Stevie "TeeVee"
1999-2001

Mistie Sioux
1991-1998

Kirby
1994-2001

Alexander "Alex"
1997-1998

Tawnee Sioux
1993-2001

Rebecca "Becca" Sioux
1991-1998

Ethan
1995-2001

Skyler "SkyeBear"
1995-1999

Jeremy
1995-2001

Thanks for finding *me* on your short journey through life—what a very special gift you were. I will always remember the beauty in each and every one of you.

Love, Mom

Fuzzbean Crossing

Ferret Angel

The Visit

Late last night,
While sound asleep,
I dreamed his whiskers
Touched my cheek.

A tickly kiss
Inside my ear;
I dreamed that he
Was very near.

I cried his name
And missed him so,
It wasn't fair
For him to go!

And in the morning
Sun so bright,
Something left
Behind last night.

Beside my pillow,
Placed with care
His favorite toy
Lay nestled there.

- Liz Blackburn

FUZZBEAN CROSSING

RAINBOW BRIDGE

The real Rainbow Bridge is the world's largest natural bridge and is located at Lake Powell, Utah. The span continues to inspire people throughout time, including the neighboring Indian tribes who consider Rainbow Bridge sacred, as well as the 300,000 people from around the world who visit it each year.

AISLYN

My Dearest Aislyn,
   I had no idea when I kissed you goodnight Sunday evening it would be for the last time. I know you didn't feel so well during the day. You ate dinner and held it down and I thought you'd be okay until morning when I took Bandit in for his surgery. If I had only known how sick you were, I never would have waited to take you. I will forever wonder if it would have made a difference. If I had done something differently, would you still be here with us? I'm so sorry that you were all alone when you died; we never got to say goodbye. You were always such a healthy little girl. I thought you'd be the one to reach your older years without the diseases that plagued your brothers and sisters. You were so young to have left so suddenly; you would have turned six in January. I still can't believe you are gone. I can only guess that Jasmine must have needed you for some mischief at the Rainbow Bridge and asked you to join her sooner rather than later. I smile to think of the two of you creating mayhem together again.
   I see you everywhere here. I see you dashing madly up the stairs with your beloved dumbbell in your mouth. I see you trying determinedly to carry a toy twice your size up the stairs, only to have it tumble back down as your reached the top, squeaking as it bounced on each step. I see you curled up in the purple ball taking a nap. I see you waking up from the soundest sleep at the slightest jingle from your dumbbell or rattle of the raisin box. I see you making your way from the staircase onto the bar to check things out. I see you sleeping with your front paws stretched forward, with you little head between them in that precious pose that only you had. I see your smudgy nose that looked like the black had worn off in spots letting the pink show through. Everywhere I look I see things you did just a few short days ago. I would never have believed that you would never do them again. I'm sorry you never got to see the pumpkin for Halloween this year. You were so cute when you tried to drag it away last year.

Fuzzbean Crossing

I hope you found the others who were waiting for you at The Bridge. Please know we miss you so much and will always love you. The room you shared with your brothers and sisters seems so empty without you and they all miss you. Your sister has taken over as keeper of the dumbbell. She has moved it into the closet and wants you to know she will take good care of it for you. Your littermate looks for you each time she wakes up, checking all the places you used to nap. She's so lost without you as we all are. Aislyn, my little girl, I will always hold you close in my heart until we meet again.

> With all my love,
> Your Mom Lucie
> Florida

Are you still using those dripping water bottles in your furball's cages? Does the water drip into the food bowl and make the ferret food soggy? Try instead the sturdy plastic bowls found in the pet store to hold food and water for birds. This type bowl goes inside the cage and has a detachable screw-type or clamp-type device that goes outside the cage to hold it firmly in place. You can find them at ferret shows also. Ferrets like drinking out of bowls better than water bottles and will drink more water each day.

ALEXANDER "ALEX"

Alex's mother was found pregnant and lost in the woods. Luckily, she was brought to my friend's ferret shelter. The kits[4] were born on May 8, 1997, and when they were old enough, they were put up for adoption. Some of them were adopted immediately, but two remained at the shelter a few weeks longer. I adopted Alex and his sister when they were four months old. At six months of age, Alex weighed a hefty five pounds.

Alex and his sister were a joy to have around and blended nicely with the other ferrets in the household. Alex was a quiet and gentle ferret.

Just one year later, in July 1998, Alex began having medical problems and had his spleen removed. His condition deteriorated and a week later he died on August 8, 1998. Alex was only 15 months old. His death was especially hard for me because he was so young and I never really got to know him well during his short life.

Love,
Mommy
Virginia

 Ah, to be a ferret and sleep in a hammock all day. That is my idea of luxury.

---

[4] Baby ferrets.

ALMOND

When I went to pick Almond up from the vet on Friday evening, I expected her to be feeling a lot better and raring to go. She had been given antibiotics and subcutaneous fluids. Whatever was going on with her, she should have been doing better than she was. The doctor told me that Almond was in kidney failure.

Almond had begun sleeping more about a week before and had slacked off on her eating. A couple of new ferrets had come into the shelter and I thought she was reacting to that. I watched her for a couple more days. She began looking scruffy and disheveled and wasn't eating. I started hand-feeding her and she began responding. I took her out of her ferret group and kept her in my bedroom. Thursday of the next week, she was visibly uncomfortable, pacing and backing into corners. The next morning we were back at the vet's for x-rays. I suspected she had a blockage and was shocked at the news I received. She had a temperature of 104° and at noon had been given antibiotics and subcutaneous fluids. The outlook was poor.

At 5:30 P.M. I called my employer at her herb shop to ask her advice. She told me to come in and get some watermelon seed tea and olive leaf extract. She also told me to give Almond enemas. Thinking that giving enemas to a squirming ferret would be a challenge, I found out it was easier than I had imagined. I also gave her more subcutaneous fluids without the antibiotics this time.

On Saturday morning I took Almond out of the carrier she had been sleeping in. She had septicemia and had not urinated since Thursday evening. I could not let her suffer and I prayed for guidance. I asked for a sign to know whether I should let her go or keep going with the treatments. I felt at peace and waited, knowing the answer would come. Amazingly, it came in five minutes. Almond walked over to the nearest corner and peed.

Through the day I continued treating her with the watermelon seed tea and olive leaf extract. I began wondering what Almond's life would be like with her kidneys so damaged. Her kidneys and bowels seemed to be working well today.

Sunday morning we went to church and I was still thinking about the damaged kidneys. Once again I prayed for guidance. When I returned home from church, I let Almond out of her carrier and she began running around as if nothing had happened. She even appeared groomed and no longer disheveled. I continued her treatment throughout the day and gave her subcutaneous fluids at bedtime. I took her to the bedroom and she began very labored breathing. I didn't know what was wrong now or even what to do next. After coming so far, she was suddenly becoming critical. The herbalist said, "When you are not sure what to do, first do nothing." Doing anything at this time for Almond would further stress her. I was so exhausted and prayed we would both fall asleep and everything would be better in the morning. During the night her breathing improved, but she was slipping away.

Monday morning I tried to feed her with a syringe and realized what was wrong. Even though Almond had been eating what I had been feeding her, her appetite was down. I thought eating lighter might lessen the stress of digestion. But that's where I made a critical mistake. Almond's nose was twitching as if she were going into a seizure. I should have been supplementing her with subcutaneous dextrose. I began doing this but she continued to slip away.

I took Almond in for an acupuncture treatment but she was comatose. I got some clematis flower essence which helps to pull one out of unconsciousness. I put the clematis under Almond's tongue and on her head, paws and bedding. She opened one eye and looked at me with a puzzled expression. I talked to her and told her whether she wanted to stay or leave, I'd be there to help her. I told her how sorry I was that I had not honed in earlier on her problem.

Throughout the day, I continued subcutaneous fluids with dextrose. Almond remained comatose and her breathing was erratic. By now I was sure her spirit wanted to free itself from this sick little body. I held her and encouraged her spirit to cross the Rainbow Bridge where there was joy and others waiting for her to come play. Almond never regained consciousness and her spirit left early Tuesday morning.

Fuzzbean Crossing

Holistic healing is about healing the body as a whole. I had become so intent on keeping Almond's kidneys functioning that I had failed to focus on the secondary damage—her decreasing and critically low blood glucose level. This was a fatal mistake and a devastating experience. I have yet another crack in my heart.

With every ferret there are lessons learned, both in life and in death.

Carol
Maryland

NOTE: Contact Carol through the author by sending e-mail to FuzzbeanCrossing@aol.com for questions or advice on herbal remedies for your ferret.

If you need to give pills to your fuzzies, put the pill in a spoon, using the back of another spoon, crush the pill and add a few drops of Ferretone or Linatone (available at pet stores). Give this pill mixture to your ferret right out of the spoon. They love it every time. If, for some reason, this doesn't work, dip your finger in the Ferretone/Linatone first and let your ferret taste this, then give the spoonful of medicine. Sometimes this works even better.

BABY

It has been a very sad week in our household. My son, Norman, had to have one of his ferrets, Baby, euthanized on his 16th birthday. Baby had been sick for about two weeks. The vet had performed several tests and surgery was done to remove a hairball. Baby seemed to perk up a little after surgery, but only for a couple of days. He then went back downhill fast.

We stopped the testing and sent him to the Rainbow Bridge when he was diagnosed with bone marrow cancer; nothing could be done to help him. The bone marrow was no longer making red blood cells and the spleen couldn't keep up. His red blood count was down to 9%.

God, watch out for a very sweet sable male ferret who is probably hogging the box of plastic eggs. Let him know how much he is missed. While we miss him dearly, we are glad he isn't suffering any more.

Linda and Norman
Kansas

Seedy-looking stools mean that your ferret's food is not being properly digested. Be a PI (Poop Inspector) and make sure this is not a regular occurrence. Stools should be smooth, not seedy or runny, and generally a nice brown color, not yellow, green or red.

BAILEY GEORGE

On October 26, 2001, at 11:30 A.M., Bailey George crossed over the Rainbow Bridge where he will join his mother and his brothers and sisters. He will run free like the wind now and have no more pain or sorrow. He will play and do his weasel war dance[5] with such pride.

Bailey George had leukemia and low blood sugar. He went in a coma and came out of it, and lost the use of his little body. We took him to the vet, but there was nothing else that could be done for him.

We thought the world of Bailey George and he will be greatly missed. Bailey was my snuggle bum; he would snuggle up with me whenever he didn't feel well. Our hearts are heavy with sadness now, even though we know he's in a better place. We will love you forever Bailey George.

Michigan

Do not use clumping cat litter in ferret litter boxes; it sticks together like cement when it gets wet. Some ferrets like to play in the litter box and could get the litter up their nose or stuck to their bottom. Either way, it could cause a blockage. Also, don't use litter that makes a lot of dust when you pour it from the bag. A good litter to use is the type made from recycled newspaper. Some people use wood stove pellets for ferret litter but the pellets are hard on soft ferret feet. Rabbit food is another good thing to use for litter. It absorbs well, is inexpensive, there is no dust, it is easy to clean up and has a nice clean smell. You can buy a 50 pound bag of rabbit food for about $10 or less at feed and farm stores. Keep the litter in a large covered plastic container so the ferrets won't dig in it and mice won't be attracted to it.

---

[5] The dance of joy that ferrets do when excited and happy.

BANDIT

It is with a heavy heart and much sadness that on December 14, 2001, I had to put my first rescued ferret to sleep. Bandit was a sweet sable male that loved everyone. He had a long life and I loved him very much. He left behind three sisters, one who was the love of his life.

Bandit had a bad heart and also suffered from insulinoma. On Friday he started having seizures and went into a coma. I took Bandit to the emergency clinic at 11:00 P.M. where he went to ferret heaven.

I always said that when Bandit died I would stop having a ferret shelter. It just hurts too much when they pass away. I haven't decided yet what I will do, but I think I will continue as long as I can help ferrets in need. I think Bandit would want it that way.

Rest in peace my friend, I love you and miss you so much. I'll see you again in another place, in another time and we will be happy together again.

Mom
Nevada

Make your own ferret hammocks and sleeping bags. You will be sure the hammocks and sleeping bags fit well in the ferret cage or sleeping area. The best materials to use are towels, child or adult sweats or baby sleepers. See instructions for making ferret hammocks and sleeping bags in the appendix.

BANDIT

God, please watch for a little sable girl named Bandit. You will know it is her because she smells like warm tortilla chips when she wakes up. She had adrenal surgery a few weeks ago but her little body just couldn't adjust. We help her to The Bridge two days later. We hope she has found her brother and three sisters who are already there. We feel so guilty for taking her in for surgery because she looked healthy. Even though she was half bald, she was so beautiful and we sure do miss her.

Thank you, God, for helping us humans adjust to the fact that their furry family members are in a safe place.

Goodbye my little potato thief.

Mom
California

When gathering trash and tying up trash bags, make sure no little pink or brown noses are around to help you. They love to climb into bags and rummage through the trash, even the dirty newspapers from the ferret room floor.

BANDIT

Hello God, it's Bella. I was wondering how my old cagemate Bandit was doing. My mom cried today because it was one year ago today that he passed over the Rainbow Bridge. We only lived with my mom three weeks before he died, but Mom is upset just the same. I know Bandit loves raisins because we came with a bunch of them. Please tell Bandit even though I have three brothers and a sister now, I miss him dearly and I'm still sleeping in our old carrying case.

> Bella
> New Jersey

Ferrets love to dig their way inside the bottom of a couch or upholstered chair. This can be hazardous because of the coils and foam rubber. To make the couch or chair secure, first make sure no one is inside and the ferrets are safely tucked away while you are working. Turn the furniture upside down and remove the thin fabric that is tacked to the bottom of the couch/chair. Staple an old bed sheet or other large piece of heavy material all around the furniture with a staple gun, sealing every opening, especially around the furniture legs. When finished, check to see that you have picked up or nailed down every tack or staple not firmly in the furniture frame and dispose of it. When the carpet sharks discover the new covering, they will undoubtedly explore every nook and cranny. They will quickly learn they can no longer get inside and find another sleeping place.

BARNABY

On a beautiful sunny day in early summer of 1994, I visited my friend's ferret shelter to look at some of the cute fuzzy kids she had recently rescued. There in the corner by the window was a basket with four furry faces looking up at me. They looked just like four little baby birds waiting for their mother to feed them. The girls had been brought into the shelter from one home and the boys from another. You could just tell they were happy being together and it certainly would not have been good to separate them. The girls were beautiful and the boys were so adorable. It didn't take very long to decide the right thing to do; pack all four of them up and head for home before I came to my senses.

The girls adjusted quickly to their new surroundings, but the boys had more difficulty. Both boys had to be handfed for a while because they became so depressed they stopped eating and drinking. Although one boy quickly decided his new home wasn't so bad, Barnaby needed more convincing. It was very hard on him for several weeks and there was a time when I wasn't sure he would manage to pull through at all. Barnaby didn't want to play or eat; he only wanted to sleep in the closet. I felt helpless as I watched his almost lifeless body just lay there. I thought he had just given up and would never eat on his own again. How do you explain to these wonderful creatures why they were given up by their former family and why they can't go home to their own bed? Luckily, one day Barnaby decided to wake up for good and join the family—finally! He became playful, happy, energetic and very comical.

One of the things that Barn liked to do was chew on the edges of rugs. The crunching was so loud; I could hear him crunching even when I was in the next room. It was so funny to watch him because he would be attacking the rug binding with his side teeth and his tongue would be hanging out of his mouth while he frantically chewed. He got great pleasure rug chewing over the years. I watched him very carefully to make sure he never bit off any of the rug or ingested anything harmful.

Barnaby also had a great trick that only he could do which was to open and close doors. It wasn't that he would just lie on his back and grab the bottom of the door with his front feet. No, it was more than that. Once he got the door open, he would stand back, get a running start and push the door closed again with his nose. He would then lie down; feet up, and open the door once again. He would play this game forever and never tired of it. I would watch him open and close and open and close the door over and over again. He was very good at it and thoroughly enjoyed playing by himself. He perfected the door closing technique so well that he once locked his sister, Becca, in the closet. He had closed the door while she was in there and the latch caught securely. From that day on, I had a plastic clothes hanger hanging on the doorknob inside the closet so Barn could never close the door tightly and trap anyone inside again.

The hair on Barnaby's body started thinning during the fall of 1997 and I had a feeling that he was beginning to show signs of adrenal disease. I fed him baby food and herbs each day and he looked forward to his nightly feeding. Just before the holidays Barn began to get weaker and lose weight. His body was not as healthy as it once had been. He was now about 6 years old. Right before Christmas, he became weaker still and was unable to walk much on his own. I put him in bed with me at night so when he attempted to get up to go to the bathroom, I would wake up and help him by holding him upright. For two and a half days, I did not leave his side.

On Sunday, December 21, 1997, at 1:05 P.M., Barnaby crossed the Rainbow Bridge. He was finally at peace. What a joy Barnaby was to me for four wonderful years, how he made me smile. I will always miss the crunching on the rug and doors silently opening and closing, as if by magic.

Goodbye my little doorman,
Mom
Virginia

BARRET

It is the ones left behind who suffer. I haven't stopped crying since the vet called me with the bad news. I hope the pain gets easier each day because right now, I feel like a huge chunk of my heart has been ripped out. Maybe it really isn't ripped; maybe it has been blessed to have had the chance to have Barret with me for as long as I did.

It was fate that brought her to my door last year. I never loved another animal like I did Barret, even though I am also the caretaker of four cats and a hamster. I would have given up my life for Barret and am sorry I was not with her when she died. I just pray she knows how much I loved her.

I used to race home to see her every day after work and I would curl up on the bed with her on weekends. This was my favorite thing to do. I will always grieve for Barret, but I am trying to be happier because I know she is at peace now.

Thank you, God, for giving me the chance to share my life with my baby Barret.

Laura
Georgia

Use a clean bowl for fresh ferret food instead of mixing it with food that's been sitting in the bowl all day. If there is any leftover food in the bowl, save it for later to mix with warm water as a tasty treat for your ferrets. If you put two bowls side by side, one with fresh food and one with day-old food, the ferrets will always eat the fresh food first.

BEANS

On January 7, 2002, our furbaby Beans crossed over the Rainbow Bridge. He was 9 years old. We are very concerned how his two cagemates will cope with the loss of their friend because they have been together their entire lives. Hobbs searched the whole house for her cagemate today. It tore my heart apart when my little Hobbs put her paws up on my leg and looked me in the eyes as if to say, "Mommy, where's my buddy?" The tears fell then.

My partner had the hardest job of all. She was the one that took Beans to the vet's office to be helped across The Rainbow Bridge. He will be missed by both of us. We loved him very much and he will always be in our hearts. Beans, you be a good boy up there.

We love you very much,
Mommy and Poppy
Indiana

You've heard of the "weasel war dance"? No, it's not the dance of joy that ferrets do when they are excited and happy, it's the dance I do when I'm getting ready for work and the weasels are biting my ankles. If anyone saw me hopping up and down on one foot at a time, they would definitely know I am doing the "weasel war dance."

BEAR

My precious Bear, a 6-year-old sable male, passed over the Rainbow Bridge last evening. I found him earlier last night sprawled under the couch with a large mass in his abdomen. I had just done my "ferret inspections" on the previous Saturday and hadn't felt anything but his enlarged spleen. This definitely wasn't his spleen.

I rushed him to the emergency clinic and they told me, "It's pretty hopeless," after just looking at him. I certainly wasn't satisfied with that, so I took Bear home. He made it through the night, and actually seemed to improve the slightest bit. I took him to our vet in the morning. The vet was slightly hopeful and said he would do exploratory surgery. I left my sweet puppy dog ferret with him and told them to call me before surgery. The veterinary technician called me later to say Bear had been given subcutaneous fluids and antibiotics. They said they were going to sedate him and would call me back when he was on the operating table. Later I received the worst news possible—an adrenal tumor had punctured his aorta.

Up to this time Bear had shown no signs of sickness or disease at all. He had no hair loss, no excessive itchiness, no change in appetite or potty habits and no sexual aggression. He was "lazy," but he'd been that way since I adopted him and his three sisters about four months ago. I rushed to the vet's office and Bear was still alive, he had waited for his Mommy. I told him I loved him and that I was very sorry, I had not known he was so sick. I talked to him about a beautiful place called the Rainbow Bridge. Afterwards, the vet helped him to The Bridge.

Regretfully, the one thing I'd never seen Bear do was the weasel war dance. Just as we were leaving the hospital, the song *I Hope You Dance* played on the radio. This made me believe my little baby, Bear, is up in the meadow running, playing and dancing his little butt off for me.

God, could you please keep an eye out for my little Bear? I have only been his Mommy for four months, but I'll love him forever.

Please tell him I love him and that I'll be looking to the skies a lot more. I'll miss you forever, Bear. Now you live in my heart instead of my house. And Bear, I hope you dance, baby, dance.

Love forever,
Mommy Lolli
Pennsylvania

 Like cats, ferrets are very clean animals and groom themselves constantly. Baths, however, are an important part of keeping ferrets clean and healthy. Once or twice a month is usually sufficient. Bathing too frequently can remove the oils from their skin and cause dry skin. Because ferrets shed their coats seasonally, it is important to remove as much of the shedding hair as possible so they don't ingest it while grooming themselves. In addition to bathing, try brushing or using a grooming glove (available at pet stores) to remove the loose fur. Unfortunately, many ferrets have surgery to remove hairballs because they usually don't throw them up like cats do. Avoid hairball problems by giving your ferret a little cat hairball remedy once a week or as necessary.

BEAR

Goodnight Bear. I cannot say goodbye, because one day I hope to see you again. Goodnight is what makes you seem closer to my heart, and my hands, which wait the day I can again cuddle you closely and smell raisins on your breath.

You were Daddy's first pick. When he saw you, he knew you were the baby for him. You were so tiny, just five weeks old. When you slept all curled up like a chocolate cinnamon roll, you could fit neatly in Daddy's hands, and still leave room for more. You were stingy with kisses, but rewarded us when you chose to give them. You loved a good rub on your tummy and you were always the first one in my lap in the morning. I will miss your winter jelly belly, your deep dark eyes so full of love, always begging to hear the sound of the raisin bag. I will miss calling out your name and having you come for a kiss and a cuddle. Most of all, I will miss your bright spirit. Of all our babies, you alone could carry the title, "Majestic," because that is who you truly were.

When you arrive at The Bridge someone will meet you to show you the way. You can dook[6] now and eat. You can walk and run and never feel another day of pain, hunger or have another seizure. I am sure you will find an unlimited supply of raisins you've always dreamed of, and you can eat them all in one day.

Today I go to pick up the furry shell you left behind. We are going to take you, your favorite sack I made and the rest of the box of raisins to a wonderful place that is filled with magic and wonder. There we will say our goodnights, tuck you in and wish angels on your pillow. Our love will always be with you. Thank you for being a wonderful part of our lives. I am grateful for the time God allowed us together. I know you will be in good company and good hands from now on. I love you Bear.

Mommy
Georgia

---

[6] The chuckling noise that ferrets make when they are happy or excited.

BETTY

Monday afternoon I took Betty to the vet where she was helped across the Rainbow Bridge. It was the hardest decision I had ever made in my life and I never want to do that again. She had been suffering from insulinoma and a liver anomaly that eventually got the best of her. She had another seizure Saturday night, but was totally unresponsive to any medication this time. She ended up at the emergency clinic that afternoon and spent the night there. Unfortunately, there was nothing I could do to save her.

Betty was 6½ years old, lived a wonderfully fun life in a loving home, and had the best dirty sock collection of any ferret. I spent three hours with her before taking her to the vet. I held her, scratched her, and gave her lots of ferret vitamins. With many tears, I said goodbye, knowing there would be no tomorrow. Her cagemate has been taking it pretty well. I took him with us to the vet, let him walk around on the table during the procedure as well as let him sniff and paw at her on my bed when I got home. He's been walking around my room looking for her and waiting patiently in his cage for her to come home.

Betty's body is now resting comfortably in a nice spot right below my bedroom window and her spirit is now waiting for us at The Bridge. She is happy again and free of pain and has all the vitamins, raisins and dirty socks she could ever want. No other animal has ever made such a profound impact on my life as a ferret and I will remember Betty always.

Chris
California

For their protection, ferrets should have rabies and distemper vaccines. It may also be a law in your state. When getting a distemper vaccine at your vet, always plan to stay a few minutes longer in the office to observe your ferret. Some ferrets have serious allergic reactions to the injection.

BO

Two days before leaving on a trip I noticed a very slight change in Bo. Although he was playing, he was not his usual "kissy" self and not quite as happy. I saw the vet the next day and we found that there was some redness around a molar—no swelling but just inflammation. He was given antibiotics and the next day I noticed some improvement. I was delighted that it didn't appear to be anything serious. The vet said that if he wasn't better in five days, he should go back for a recheck. I definitely agreed; we didn't want to lose the tooth. I was so relieved because I didn't want to go out of town knowing that one of these little guys might be sick. As I told my ferretsitter, "no one dies of a toothache."

When my ferretsitter picked me up at the airport she took my hand in hers and, trembling, told me that my little Bo had died. I felt my heart clench and I could hardly understand what she was saying. She had taken him back to the vet two days after I left because he wasn't doing well. The vet found a blood clot in his stomach. I'm not sure if the tooth problem had anything to do with it or somehow masked the real problem. Perhaps it was a coincidence and Bo had two unrelated problems. I will always regret not being there for him.

I miss Bo dearly and am so very sad. He was just 4½ years old and was known as the "mad kisser." He gave big sloppy kisses as a kit, the kind dogs give, and would move his whole head up and down. When he lay in my arms and I rubbed his back, he would keep giving kisses until my cheek turned red.

I was Bo's favorite toy; he preferred playing with me rather than with the other ferrets. Bo was a sweet and beautiful "mama's boy" with great big eyes. I'm fortunate some beautiful photographs have been taken of him. He was the cowboy for the cover of the 1999 Ferret Calendar and Sherlock Holmes on the 2001 calendar cover. I will remember him most for his affection, his eager and cherished little face and his happy silvermitt dance of joy.

Virginia

BONES

God, it is with a heavy heart and tears of pain that I write this letter to you. Our Bones crossed The Bridge yesterday with the help of the vet. Bones was so weak, so fragile, and so slim. He'd lost so much weight and nothing we tried would help him gain it back.

Yesterday I let him out to run with the others and he had difficulty using his legs. He dragged himself around the house and pooped on himself. I couldn't bear to watch him suffer this way anymore.

That afternoon Bones and I crawled into the car and went to the hospital. We stopped along the way to get a chocolate shake for him. What could it hurt? He loved it and lapped it from the straw. He sat on my lap in his sleep sack for the entire ride. Just before we made it to the hospital, I realized I hadn't told Bones about the Rainbow Bridge. I took a few moments in private with him to let him know about the "other side."

Bones was one of the first rescues the shelter ever did. I think he was now ready to leave, but it didn't make it any easier for me. I held him in my arms and told him I loved him as tears poured down my face.

This will be the last time you hurt, my little guy. I love you Bones, sleep well.

Missing you already,
Mom
Canada

BONES

My ferret, Bones, passed away Sunday night a little after 11 o'clock. He was 8 years old. Bone was my first ferret; I got him when he was just a kit and I was 16 years old. Bones and I have been through a lot together; he gave me eight years of love, laughs, happiness and company. He loved to go outside in his harness and would snorkel in the grass. He loved plastic bags and emptying purses and would curl up and sleep in them. He was the cup-tipping champion and could smell Mountain Dew a mile away. When he was 2 years old, his favorite game was to trap me in the kitchen, run at me, jump as high up my legs as he could and slide down. He knew I had nowhere to run.

He had been more active than usual this last month, showing no signs of problems. He spent a lot of time with me in the living room. He enjoyed coming out of the ferret room and would run around the house. He began having problems walking Sunday and progressively got worse throughout the day. He only ate small amounts of chicken baby food mixed with Pedialyte[7]. He perked up a little when I offered him Ferretone[8], but this time he didn't lick my hand clean like he usually did.

Bones passed away in my arms and I was happy I was holding him. This is the first ferret I've lost and I had lived with Bones longer than any other pet I've had. I will miss my Bones. The other ferrets will miss him also and have been looking for him.

God, please watch for Bones. He won't know anyone there, so show him around if you have time. He loves ferret vitamins and raisins. Tell him his mommy loves him and misses him.

Micaela
Indiana

---

[7] An electrolyte liquid that is available from grocery and drug stores usually in the infant section. It is given to ferrets suffering from dehydration.

[8] Ferret vitamin supplement available at pet supply stores.

BOOGER

Dear God,

I knew the day would come when I would have to ask you to greet one of our babies. Could you please watch out for our beautiful little girl Booger? She will be the dark sable girl with the dark eyes. She is a sweet little girl who is 7¾ years old and loves to give kisses. Please show her where the raisins, the red licorice and the ferret vitamins are, because these are her favorite treats. She is our first to go and has no one there to meet her. She may be a little scared and nervous and won't know where to go. Once she gets to know you, she can be a little bossy at times.

Booger left us this morning somewhere between 2:00-4:00 A.M. I kept a small light on to keep from falling asleep but I guess I did anyway. When I looked over at Booger, I realized she was gone. Last night I had her in bed with me wrapped in blankets to keep her warm. I cuddled her and put my arms around her so she knew she wasn't alone. Booger became sick just before Christmas and we found out she had an ulcer. Booger died from liver failure and she was losing her hair due to adrenal disease. She was with us for a little over two years.

In the beginning I didn't know how much love and joy ferrets could bring into your life. When we got our first ferret we realized he was lonely and soon got a second and then a third. Now I can't imagine my life without them because they bring so much joy and happiness each and every day.

Booger was our third and came to live with us in May 1999. When she first arrived at our home and was let her out of her carrying cage, she started to war dance like crazy and make all kinds of sounds. She was so happy to be running around free because she had not had much playtime at her last home. She loved to curl up on your chest, crawl down your sleeve, pop her head out the other end. Sometimes she would just stay there curled up and fall asleep. If you were lying down, she would crawl up your pant leg and go to sleep there, too. She would even curl up around your neck. She loved to give lots of kisses and it was lick, lick, lick, and then a little chomp. During the past year, she had been doing more kissing and less chomping. I will miss this most about her; she was my kissy girl.

My heart aches for my little girl. She has taken a piece of my heart with her to Rainbow Bridge and I hope she hangs onto it and waits for us all there. God, please tell our little girl how sorry we are and that we tried to help her. Tell her we hope she is not angry at us, but we never knew until late last night how sick she really was. We have so many wonderful memories and photographs of Booger that we will treasure always. We love you, my sweet little princess, and now you can rest peacefully until we all meet again.

Mommy, Daddy and Michael
Canada

Does your ferret scratch their ears a lot or rub their head on the carpet frequently? Those cute little pink fuzzy ears may contain ear mites. When you clean the ears, look for dark brown/black specks in the earwax which could mean an ear mite problem.

Take your ferret to the vet for closer inspection. If your ferret has ear mites, your vet will recommend either ear drops or an injection. If one of your furries gets ear mites, all your ferrets will need to be treated to get rid of the problem. Change the ferret bedding frequently to help alleviate ear mites.

BREANNA LYNN

God, please watch for my baby BreAnna Lynn; she left me Tuesday night. I think she wanted to be with her Grandpa Jack at the Rainbow Bridge. BreAnna had been fighting insulinoma since January 2000, and I rushed her to the emergency room on Tuesday. I thought she might be extremely low on her blood glucose count. The doctors put her on an IV and took x-rays. She started to perk up a little overnight, but I got the call this morning saying she had left for the Rainbow Bridge to look for her Grandpa.

I can't quit crying for her. God, please tell her I love her and miss her deeply. Her brother and I will join her one day. Please make sure there are extra Cheerios on hand for her arrival.

Love always,
Mommy
Ohio

Leave the ferrets at home with a reliable ferret sitter if you are vacationing at the beach in the middle of summer. Ferrets do not tolerate temperatures over 80° and need to be in a more comfortable environment. Better yet, go to the beach in the fall when it is cooler and take the carpet sharks along. Remember to pack the ferret harnesses and leashes.

Albino and Sable Friends

THE RAINBOW BRIDGE
Inspired by a Norse Legend

By the edge of a woods, at the foot of a hill,
Is a lush, green meadow where time stands still.
Where the friends of man and woman do run,
When their time on earth is over and done.

For here, between this world and the next,
Is a place where each beloved creature finds rest.
On this golden land, they wait and they play,
Till the Rainbow Bridge they cross over one day.

No more do they suffer, in pain or in sadness,
For here they are whole, their lives filled with gladness.
Their limbs are restored, their health renewed,
Their bodies have healed, with strength imbued.

They romp through the grass, without even a care,
Until one day they start, and sniff at the air.
All ears prick forward, eyes dart front and back,
Then all of a sudden, one breaks from the pack.

For just at that instant, their eyes have met;
Together again, both person and pet.
So they run to each other, these friends from long past,
The time of their parting is over at last.

The sadness they felt while they were apart,
Has turned into joy once more in each heart.
They embrace with a love that will last forever,
And then, side by side, they cross over... together.

- Steve and Diane Bodofsky

BUBBY

God, please welcome our little fuzzy, Bubby. He passed over the Rainbow Bridge this morning after losing his battle with diabetes.

Bubby was our sweet little baby who would follow us all over the house and never caused any problems. Please help him find his sister and brothers who preceded him to The Bridge. His remaining brothers and sister miss him terribly, as do his Mommy and Daddy. Can you also direct him to the Cheerios and Ferrevite[9]? These were his favorites. Thanks.

Dan
Massachusetts

Pick up sleeping ferrets gently, especially when they are curled up or sleeping upside down with their head between their back feet. Although they sometimes wake up quickly, you want to make sure not to injure their back by "unwinding" them from the curled position. Use both hands around the body until they are fully awake and stretch themselves out lengthwise.

---

[9] Ferret vitamin supplement available at pet supply stores.

BUCKWHEAT
October 1994 - February 25, 2002

Buckwheat came into our lives with his brothers Alfalfa and Spanky. Originally, Bucky was to go to a friend of ours and the others would stay with us. Buckwheat wouldn't eat while our friend kept him so he came back to live with us. He had to be force fed every four hours around the clock for a long time. One day we went on a picnic and took Bucky along with us. Someone dropped a piece of brownie; Buckwheat found it and devoured it. He soon began eating other foods after this.

Buckwheat lost his brothers in 1999 and in 2000. Their passing didn't seem to affect him as he had made other friends here. He had a passion for frosted Cheerios and would do just about anything for one. Buckwheat began showing signs of adrenal disease last year. He had surgery in the fall to remove a growth on the front of his shoulder. In the past few weeks, his health declined and we finally had to make the decision to help him over the Rainbow Bridge. As difficult as this decision was, I am happy knowing that the Little Rascals are all together once again.

Minnesota

Never leave a dishwasher door standing open because ferrets love to climb inside to drink the water left at the bottom. Pull the latch all the way closed; otherwise they can still open the door. Ferrets can easily be overlooked when the door is closed and get locked inside. Check once, check again and one more time before securing the door or washing dishes.

BUDDY

My beloved ferret, Buddy, passed away this morning at the age of two. Although he was deaf, blind and had an enlarged heart, he was the sweetest ferret I've ever met.

He got sick yesterday afternoon and, by the early hours of this morning, he was gone. I miss him so much. I only had him for less than twelve months.

God, please keep him in your thoughts and I hope he finds some friends up there over the Rainbow Bridge. Thanks.

Naomi
Australia

Even though your ferret may be blind, they can get around quite well. Sometimes it's difficult to tell whether a ferret is blind just by observing them. If they occasionally bump into furniture or walls, they are probably blind. Give handicapped fuzzy ones a little extra time and attention each day. They deserve it and you'll be happy you did.

BUDDY

Dear God,
  Have you seen Buddy up there yet? He should have arrived about a week ago. His pal, Franky, is already there. I think Buddy missed Franky so much that he had to cross The Bridge to be with his friend. Buddy hadn't even been sick, but I think he died of a broken heart because he and Franky had grown up together. Buddy was a cute and docile ferret who loved to steal socks.
  Tell Bud that I laid him beside Franky so they will be together forever. And one more thing, God, be sure to tell them both how much I love and miss them.

>   Susan
>   Iowa

 Take off your shoes while the ferrets are running freely around the house. You cannot feel tiny ferret feet under yours if wearing shoes or slippers. Watch where you step, there could be a ferret under your foot. They are always underfoot and under rugs and under that pile of dirty laundry in the corner. Be extremely cautious where you step, especially if your ferret has an enlarged spleen. Stepping on your ferret could possibly rupture the spleen.

BUTTERCUP

Buttercup died on Saturday, May 12, 2001, around noon. She was over 7 years old. On Friday evening, we realized the end was near. On Saturday morning, she had not moved from her pouch all night. She refused food and made little groans. She died in the vet's waiting room while I held her.

Buttercup was a pretty little sable ferret with a cute pointed nose and a very bright expression. She was very smart. Some of her favorite toys were little footballs of crinkle material sewn around some stuffing. Buttercup held these toys beneath her and used them like a sled to slide down the ramp between the floors of the cage. When she got to the bottom she would pick up the toy, carry it up and do it over again. This was very amusing to watch.

A maze of clear dryer hose runs around the perimeter of our ferret room. Buttercup used to chase the other ferrets through this maze. Buttercup would exit the maze, run across the room, and reenter the maze from the other side of the room. This enabled her to cut the other two off and ambush them. Buttercup was an expert in running nearly full speed backwards inside a dryer hose.

After the other two ferrets died, Buttercup started putting little stuffed animals inside any available ferret tent or sleeping pouch. She liked these animals so much, we kept buying her more. Her favorites were Curious George, a set of mice, and small finger puppets. Often, she would put away ten or fifteen of these toys in one session.

Buttercup's strong will brought her through many crises during her three-year battle with adrenal cancer. She lived nearly two and one-half years longer than we expected. She continued to eat "soup"[10] on her own the day before she died, and she was putting her favorite stuffed animals in her sleeping pouch last week.

---

[10] This is a reference to "duck soup." See page 69 for explanation.

Buttercup is survived by three others whose cage is now full of Buttercup's collection of little stuffed animals.

In Maryland the buttercups have been blooming since the first of May. Our Buttercup survived one last buttercup season. The next time you see a field of buttercups blooming, please remember her.

Bill and Clare
Maryland

 To find free-roaming ferrets lost in the house, stop, look and listen. Turn down the TV or other noise, look in their usual hiding and/or sleeping places and listen. Do you hear any stirring, scratching or other movement? Ferrets usually tend to sleep or hide in the same location. Once you know these places, this should be where you look first. Train them to respond to a squeaky toy or sound. Make the sound and give them a treat such as Cheerios. Repeat this training frequently so they associate the treat with the sound and will come when you need them to. Just shaking the Cheerios container usually gets ferrets running. If your ferret sleeps very soundly, as they tend to, the sound may not wake them up. Be prepared to remove cushions, move furniture, and get down on your hands and knees to look under the sofa to locate the missing ferret. Especially look in boxes, open drawers, or other possible hiding areas where a ferret could curl up to sleep.

CAEL

My Cael boy has gone to The Bridge. He was getting sicker over the last weeks, with no hope coming home from the doctor. I had made the decision today to help him along to the Rainbow Bridge. I waited for a call back from my vet all afternoon, but discovered the message wasn't given to him before he left. I sat at my desk at work and cried on the phone with my mother about having to make this choice. When I arrived home from work, only four ferrets could be found. My heart stopped, and I knew. I searched and searched, but couldn't find Cael anywhere. Finally, I looked in one of my dryer tubes. This was Cael's favorite toy when he was young. At some point he got too fat for the smaller tube and stopped going in it. Today, this is where I found him. His nose was barely poking out; he was looking content as though he was asleep in his favorite spot. But he wasn't just sleeping.

I buried him in his favorite cozy bed, still in the tube. I put alongside him his hacky sack and a note from a friend. He is buried in the yard and there are blue flowers on top of his grave.

God, please look for Cael. He will be carrying a yellow hacky sack with a smiley face on it.

Melissa
Nebraska

Signs of illness or concern: disheveled look (fur out of place, especially around the head and neck area), bad breath or other unusually strong smell, deep-set and lifeless eyes, weakness, trembling, grinding teeth, increased respiratory rate. These are all signs that you should get your ferret checked thoroughly at the vet.

CAESAR

God, would you please keep an eye out for my little Caesar? She had been sick the last few days and I was going to take her to the doctor today, but I guess she just didn't want to stay around any longer. We weren't sure of her age but figured she was at least 6 years old. She had an adrenal gland removed over two years ago and had insulinoma for two years, which she was handling well. She had just received her second Lupron[11] injection a couple of months ago and was scheduled to have her second adrenal gland removed soon. She was proud of the new fur coat she was growing, especially the little black tip of her tail, since she was a dark-eyed white-colored ferret.

God, tell her I'm sorry I didn't catch whatever it was that caused her to get sick this past weekend. I wish I had known how bad she was feeling. Maybe she just figured she was getting old and didn't want to fight any longer. At least she was with me when she left, she knew I loved her and she wasn't alone or scared. She has four brothers and one sister already at The Bridge. Caesar is bringing two small boxes of raisins to share with her brothers and sister. She loved to wrestle and hide under blankies and sacks. Maybe she can find some up there to play with. Tell Caesar I love her and miss her so much. Tell the rest of them I'm still thinking about all of them, too, and for them to make Caesar feel at home. Thank you so much God.

MJO
Arizona

---

[11] See the appendix for a description of this medication.

CALLIE

My little fighter is gone. Callie came to us as a rescue with an advanced case of adrenal disease. My vet and I didn't think she'd make it, but she did and even regrew a lush orange coat. She was an albino, but I don't think the color of her coat mattered to her, she was just so happy to have hair.

We took a short vacation trip last week, and while we were gone, she stopped eating and started showing signs of insulinoma. We tried Cortisone[12], set the alarm every two hours to feed her, but nothing worked and she went downhill very fast.

Yesterday we let her go. She was so tiny and we held her, kissed her and sent her on her way. My heart is breaking. I blame myself for being away those few days. It might have made a difference and I'm afraid I added needlessly to her suffering. I can't forgive myself.

When I got my cancer diagnosis, her fortitude inspired me. Both of us were sick, but still determined to live. She was doing so well, but suddenly experienced a downturn. It was scary. I miss her so much; she was very special.

I'm generally not religious, God, but I'm asking you to please say a prayer for Callie. I hope she's not hurting anymore. Ask her to forgive me for not being there last week.

Kym
Kentucky

---

[12] See the appendix for a description of this medication.

CASSIDY SIOUX

It was May 1994 when I adopted four fuzzies who were nestled close together in a little basket at the ferret shelter. As I looked down into the basket, they looked like four tiny baby birds. Adopting four at once was a big decision, but since they had already bonded with each other, I did not want to separate them. All four were such a delight over the years and fit in wonderfully with all the other ferrets in the household.

Cassidy Sioux was a quiet little sable girl all her life and never demanded attention like some of the more aggressive ferrets I've lived with. Sometimes I felt she got a little neglected because she didn't constantly demand my attention. I spent extra time with her whenever I could so she would know how much she was loved. One thing she couldn't get enough of was Cheerios and would gobble them up as fast as I could feed them to her.

Cassie lost most of her hair in 1998 and was diagnosed with adrenal disease. She was given Lupron injections instead of having surgery and looked so cute when she was regrowing her new coat. When Cassie Sioux died on October 22, 1999, she was 6 or 7 years old.[13]

Mom
Virginia

Save large padded mailing envelopes with bubble wrap inside (they come this way). This makes a great toy for your ferret. They love to crawl inside and pop the bubbles. Watch them carefully, and throw the bag away when the plastic gets shredded. This way, none of the plastic particles get swallowed.

---

[13] See Barnaby's, Rebecca Sioux's and Sandie's stories elsewhere in the book.

CHANDLER

Today I must endure the devastating pain of losing our "first born" ferret friend. Chandler Bing, our "yawn boy" died this evening. We are all very upset by this sudden event.

Almost three years ago, Chandler picked Louis and me out at a pet store in Washington. We fell in love with him immediately. He was gentle, even as a kit, and only opened his mouth to eat or yawn. That is why we nicknamed him "Yawn Boy." He loved to go for walks and dig in the dirt. On occasion we offered mice to the ferrets. This was accepted by most of them as a wonderful treat. But Chandler, being his gentle self, could not kill the mice. He would, instead, take them away from the others and put them in the food bowl, but not to eat. He wanted to make sure everything was in its place, and he knew this was the place for the mice.

God, please ensure that Chandler's brothers and sister meet him on the other side of the Rainbow Bridge. Chandler was deaf, so please let him hear us for the first time when we look up and say, "We love you." Take care of our fuzzy friend. Chandler was a true ambassador for ferrets. Only Chandler could bring a smile to your face while washing his. We love you Chandler.

Always and forever,
June and Louis
Kentucky

If you are thinking about purchasing a new cage for your ferret, make sure it is large enough for them to move around freely inside. Your ferret should be able to stand upright in the cage. Add a hammock, a litter box, some food and water and you have a comfortable place where your fuzzmittens are safe until you let them out to play.

CHEROKEE

Cherokee was 3½ years old and the fattest ferret you've ever seen, all four pounds of her. So chubby, she would roll over when she tried to wash herself. Even though she made us laugh, she was not a nice ferret. She was a nose, hand, and toe biter and she meant business. But I loved her anyway. She was a Canadian ferret with a bad attitude.

She began to have seedy stools without blood or diarrhea. After having her examined, she was given every drug you could imagine from Amoxicillin[14] to Carafate[15] to an ulcer combination. She began to lose weight and I was getting very worried. She still ate with gusto and still tried to bite my nose.

Cherokee was taken again to the vet who took a barium x-ray. It appeared that her lymph nodes were very swollen. The vet wanted to do exploratory the next day. The barium just wasn't passing all the way through. I thought maybe my big "garbanzo bean" ate something bad or had a hairball. I left her at the vet's office the next day and never got to see her alive again. The vet found stomach cancer plus the start of insulinoma. The vet said recovery would be long and hard, if she even recovered at all. I regret that I never got to say goodbye.

Joan
Ohio

---

[14] See the appendix for a description of this medication.
[15] See the appendix for a description of this medication.

CHICKY

I lost my first ferret last Saturday; her name was Chicky. Chicky came into my life when I went to our local shelter to get a kit. I picked out my new little girl and the shelter mom asked me if I wanted to foster a sick ferret. I ended up bringing home two little girls instead of one. Chicky was almost bald and had a tumor on her tail, but she was very spunky and bright eyed. When I brought her home, I told my husband we probably would not have her very long. She was, after all, a sick little girl.

Although she slept more than my other ferrets, she ran everywhere when she was awake. She never walked, just ran. As time went on, she spent more time out of her cage and even started eating on her own. She didn't like being held and she didn't like other ferrets. Occasionally, I would catch her doing "ferret things" like sniffing in shoes and bags. This little girl never danced, never dooked, never played—she just ran. I loved her with all my heart even though she was technically still a shelter ferret. She was a big part of our family and stayed with us for almost one year. Last week, she started losing weight. She wanted to be held and would come over to the couch to stand by my foot and touch me with her nose. When I picked her up, she fell asleep on my lap.

On Friday, Chicky stopped eating and, by that evening, she could not use her front and back legs. I called the shelter and the decision was made to help her over The Bridge the next day. The last time I saw her was in the vet's office, her little bald head sticking out of her favorite sleep sack.

I loved you, Chicky, and did all I could to let you know you were loved. I know she will now be able to dance, dook and play whenever she wants to do. Now she will have a full coat and no tumor on her tail. When I returned home from the vet's office, I hugged my other four fuzzies for what they thought was way too long. I plan to do that everyday from now on.

Laura
Georgia

CHOMPER

My oldest boy, Chomper, has crossed the Bridge. I can't even cry right now, all I feel is numbness.

I got Chomper from a pet store in April 1996. He was always laid back, very mellow and never gave me a minute's worth of trouble. He ate whatever food I was currently trying without a fuss, and knew what the litter box was for from the first time he saw it. During playtime, he was content to wander for a while and then come back to cuddle. His favorite toys were stuffed animals, it didn't matter what kind. When we brought home the second ferret, Chomper welcomed her and they quickly bonded. They remained cagemates for three years.

Chomper left us suddenly one day and his cagemate looked rather puzzled, as if she couldn't understand why Chomper wasn't playing. I now will lavish lots of attention on the remaining little girl so she won't feel Chomper's absence too much.

God, please watch out for Chomper. He will arrive carrying a stuffed animal and his blanket. He is really partial to sweet tea, so if there is any sweet tea up there, please show him where it is. Also, look up his two buddies and have them meet him at The Bridge. Buddy will be glad to see his brother once again.

Chompie, we miss you baby; you are now a shining star. Run, sweet boy, and play to your heart's content. Mommy will see you when she gets to The Bridge. I love you so very much, my sweet little boy.

Pat
North Carolina

CHUCK

God, please help Chuck find his buddies up there. Chuck had insulinoma and had been on medication for three months. One week ago he didn't want to eat, then on Monday began having black, sticky, tarry diarrhea. I had to force feed him and give him his medications. He also had a bloody nasal discharge. Monday he went to the vet and was put on more medication. On Tuesday he was back at the vet for subcutaneous fluids. He seemed to do better for a few days, but still not eating on his own. A friend contacted his vet who said it sounded like DIC[16], which I'd never heard of, but was given a detailed description on how to recognize it. On Thursday I noticed Chuck had DIC splotches on his body, and was immediately rushed to the vet. I told the vet tech if there was anything they could do, please do so; if not, to just keep him comfortable until I could get back to him at 5:00 P.M.

After getting back to the vet office, I talked to Chuck while waiting for the vet. I'd talked to the vet and she suggested that I have him euthanized, as DIC usually kills within twenty-four hours. Chuck was a deaf blaze ferret who would have been 5 years old in February 2002. I know he couldn't hear me telling him about the Rainbow Bridge, yet I hoped he felt the vibrations of love I was sending him. I held Chuck while he crossed The Bridge.

A necropsy was done and it was found that Chuck had tumors on his enlarged spleen, liver tumors, pancreatic tumors and tumors on the lymph nodes in his chest cavity.

Chuck, I'm so sorry you had to leave, yet I'm so hopeful you didn't have to suffer long. Wait for me, babies; we'll all be together in the future.

Your loving Mom,
Sandi
Texas

---

[16] Dissemination Intravascular Coagulation (DIC) is the blood's inability to clot.

CHUCKIE

In December 1993, I received a phone call from my real estate agent who knew I had ferrets. She mentioned that her son was looking for a new home for his ferret. I drove the sixty miles to the next state to look at the ferret and consider bringing him home.

When I arrived at their house, it appeared that this family enjoyed the company of the family dog who lived well in the house, but the ferret was banished to the unused and cold garage. He was living alone in a small filthy cage, with a dirty hammock and litter box that had not been cleaned in a very long time. There was no one to talk to him, no one to play with him and no one to pay any attention to his needs. Chuckie was 3 years old at the time, and I didn't want to ask if he had lived his entire life in this disgusting and unhealthy environment. I had no choice but to get Chuckie away from his lonely existence and home to the other two ferrets living in the household.

Chuck adapted quickly to his new home and free-roaming lifestyle. There were no more cages, no more dirty litter boxes and there was plenty of fresh food and water. He also got lots of attention and had other furry "people" like himself to play with and he soon became a very outgoing ferret. One of his favorite things to do was to pick on the girl ferrets, all except Mistie. He absolutely adored her and would cuddle up with her whenever possible.

One day Chuckie summoned his courage enough to jump on the "alpha" ferret of the group, who was always extremely docile. The dominant ferret quickly and silently pinned Chuckie to the floor and gave him a good hard bite on the neck. Chuckie got up unscathed, shook himself off, and walked away quickly as if he was embarrassed and hoping no one else had seen what had just taken place. He obviously did not want to tarnish his "tough guy" image.

In January 1999, at over 8 years old, he was operated on for insulinoma. For the next few months, Chuckie slept a lot and never did quite bounce back to an active lifestyle after his surgery. He was an old timer for a ferret and, over the next few months, his health declined. On June 3, 1999, Chuckie crossed the Rainbow Bridge.

He had managed to live longer than any of the other ferrets I've lived with and had a very happy and comfortable life for six of his eight or nine years. You can't ask for much more than that.

His grave marker in the backyard says: *Chuckie, 1990-1999, What a Great Life!*

> I love you my big man,
> Mom
> Virginia

Instead of using a standard urn for ashes after having your ferret cremated, spend a day at the mall shopping for a special container just for them. Choose something meaningful that complements their personality. Look for brass, copper, wood or even decorative plastic containers. Think of having a brass, copper or wood container engraved with your ferret's name. You can even get an inexpensive wood burning tool and personalize a wooden box yourself. If the container cannot be engraved, purchase a separate metal tag to engrave and glue permanently to the container. This type of container you choose for your ferret is much less expensive than a standard urn and so special because you spent the time finding just the right thing. Think of what a great healing experience for your heart this will be.

CLYDESDALE "CUBBY"

In November 1995, a friend called and said she had just received a great big boy ferret at her ferret shelter. I was interested because I've always been partial to large male ferrets. There was only one problem with this young boy—he was a biter.

I went to the shelter to see him and he was gorgeous, but aren't they all! I had to laugh when I saw his feet because he had the biggest and hairiest feet I had ever seen on a ferret. My friend had aptly named him Clydesdale, after the huge Clydesdale horses. This was a perfect name for him. He had already bitten a couple of people since he had arrived at the shelter, as well as his former veterinarian. I decided I would adopt him even though I knew he would be a challenge.

After bringing him home I bathed him to get him ready for his new home. He managed to get a hold of my hand and gave me a nasty bite almost through to the bone. Ouch, that hurt!

For a few days I kept him isolated in a separate room from the other ferrets as I always do with the new ferrets. And, if the truth were known, I was afraid of getting too close to him. For days I spent time on and off in the room with Clydesdale, sitting in a chair out of his reach. I wore hightop shoes with heavy socks and long heavy pants when I went in there, just in case. I wasn't taking any chances on getting bit again. I wanted him to get used to me. I was not aggressive towards him in any way; I just sat there and quietly talked to him while he listened and observed me. While spending time with this new ferret I thought about what I could call him. Clydesdale wasn't one of those names that rolled off the tongue easily. I decided to nickname him Cubby, which worked just fine.

After four days of just sitting in the room with Cubby, I decided I did not want to spend all my time afraid of this little creature. I decided to pick him up and hold him. I was wearing a long sleeved shirt at the time, of course. Magically, this was the start of a wonderful relationship. From this moment, he never tried to bite me again and I could tell he really enjoyed being held. To this day, he was the ferret that wanted the most love and attention of all the

Fuzzbean Crossing

other ferrets. He had such a sweet personality. Perhaps something unpleasant had happened to him before I knew him and he had no recourse but to defend himself by biting. Although he was very loving to me, I never trusted him totally around anyone else because a couple of times he tried to bite people who came to the house.

Cubby wasn't the healthiest ferret and battled allergies most of his life, having a dry itchy coat and skin and red swollen eyes. He spent much time getting checked at the doctor. Early in 1999, it was thought that Cubby had adrenal disease because he was losing tail hair. Through exploratory surgery, an inoperable tumor was found and he was sent home to rest comfortably. He managed to be comfortable for many weeks. On November 6, 2000, Cubby developed breathing problems and died at only 5 years old.

One of the things I remember most about Cubby was his large, perfectly round head. It was the perfect shape for stroking as I cuddled him against my shoulder. I will always remember the wonderful hugs we shared and the very loving relationship we had. Cubby was such a special ferret.

Mommy
Virginia

 On a rainy Sunday afternoon when all the carpet surfers are asleep, why not play a game of "ferret" Scrabble®. Make words that are ferret-related such as furry, dook, kiss, or cuddle, etc. What fun!

COLONEL SANDERS

I have been rescuing and fostering ferrets for well over one year. Sometimes a ferret will come to you and embed themselves into your heart. This was the case with Colonel Sanders.

The local Humane Society called and I went to pick up a beautiful silver boy with a white face and breath that made you gag. His gums looked swollen, and his breath was so bad I had to drive with the car window open.

I took him to my friend's ferret shelter. She brought out a tooth-cleaning pick and started to investigate the mouth problem. It didn't take long before she had to stop to keep from gagging. I put some perfume under both our noses, thinking that would help. She found compacted food between the gums that looked like shredded chicken. She picked and irrigated, exposing irritated gums all around. Needless to say, she fell in love with this little boy and named him Colonel Sanders. After taking Colonel Sanders to the vet clinic, he recovered completely. He was the sweetest, cuddliest little guy with a wonderful disposition who was loved immensely.

I visited my friend recently and she mentioned Colonel Sanders was looking old lately, older than she had originally thought. I was fortunate to spend some time with him while I was there. This morning I received an e-mail message from her saying, "I just wanted to let you know that Colonel Sanders passed away sometime yesterday. When I came home from work and found him, it looked like he was just sleeping. I think he died from old age. It's been very hard for me."

Michigan

CUSTARD

As a result of the findings of exploratory surgery and the recommendation of the vet, Custard, known to her loved ones as "Cussieweezil," was helped across the Rainbow Bridge. We wrote this poem for her.

CUSSIEWEEZIL

You gave so much so freely, in your special little way
Until the time arrived that you would have to go away
Your voice now stilled forever your eyes no longer see
No longer will my baby girl, wardance her way 'round me.

The gift you gave so freely in your loving little way
Will stay with us forever, it did not die this day
We lost our Cussieweezil, fate said it must be so
A brief farewell, a tender kiss, and then you had to go.

So rest in peace my baby, safe now from the pain
Nothing now can hurt you, you can be free again
Our little Custard angel, well miss you every day
And always will regret the fact you had to go away.

Cris and Lee
West Wales
United Kingdom

DAKOTA "KOTI" TBEAR

Koti's favorite game was playing with little green squeaky frogs. Each day when Koti got up from his nap, he would stand on his back legs and look up over the top and down into a carpeted cat play tube in the hallway to see if there were any frogs inside. If he found one—he usually did—he would lower himself down into the tube and hang with his feet hooked up over the top. All I could see was his two little feet hanging over the edge. Down he would go to catch the frog. He carried it carefully in his mouth and ran as fast as he could to hide it behind the bed. He usually had quite a stash of frogs back there. Periodically, I would round up the frogs from behind the bed so Koti would have plenty more to find in the tube. He never tired of this game, even when he was not feeling well during the last month.

Koti loved to climb up the front of my pants leg when I was standing in the kitchen. He wanted to climb on the counter to convince me he needed a treat from the treat jar. He would look at me with those beautiful brown eyes and push the treat jar over to me. I could never resist his charms and he always got a little treat. Each time another ferret was adopted, they bonded with Koti right away and they loved him very much.

In late December Koti was diagnosed with kidney failure and, soon afterward, a heart murmur was discovered. He stayed in the hospital for several days getting medication, subcutaneous fluids, and a special diet. Bloodwork was done each week. I hoped his weekly tests would show Koti was getting better. However, that's not the way it happened. I consulted several "ferret" doctors including a vet pathologist, homeopathic vet, and a cardiologist who all read the bloodwork and said the outlook did not look encouraging. I tried to make Koti as comfortable as possible during January and would handfeed him, talk to him, hold him and let him sleep inside my sweatshirt while I sat on the couch comforted in his closeness. The other ferrets took turns sleeping with Koti during his sickness to keep him warm and secure. Each day, however, I saw no improvement and could tell he was losing weight and wasting away. Koti stayed in my bedroom where he slept right beside my bed so I could be there for him. I even put his frogs close to him so he could find them easily and not have to carry them too far.

During his last days Koti lost interest in food, water and even his frogs. I put him in bed with me that night and let him sleep and warmed him on my stomach with my T-shirt wrapped around him. He seemed quite comforted by this. During the night I made the hardest decision I'll ever have to make—to end Koti's suffering. I made an appointment with his doctor the next morning.

On Friday, February 2, 1996, at 12:50 P.M., Dakota TBear "Koti" crossed the Rainbow Bridge for happier times. I never thought Koti would leave so soon; he was not yet 3 years old. It was way too soon for him to go and leave us behind, but I guess God had special plans for him.

My precious beloved BearBear, I tried so hard to make you better and to protect you throughout your short life. I'm so sorry there wasn't anything left I could do. You will be missed more than words can express and I hope there are lots of little green frogs in heaven for you to catch. Goodbye, my brave little man.

Mommy
Virginia

Weigh your carpet sharks once a month to make sure no one is losing or gaining more than a couple of ounces here and there. If your ferret loses weight quickly, consult with your vet to rule out any medical problems. Weigh them at the same time each month and write it on a chart so you will be able to compare the weights from month to month. You can buy an inexpensive kitchen scale for under $10 at one of the discount department stores. A sample weight chart can be found in the appendix.

DEMENTIA "DEMI" SIOUX

She was my first ferret and a beautiful dark-eyed white color. I acquired Demi and her cagemate in 1992 from my son who no longer had time to care for them. My son was a veterinary technician at the time and lived with a variety of animals. I knew nothing about ferrets then, but thought they were very cute. It was a learning experience for me that continues even today. I learned that I had to ferret-proof the house; I learned what insulinoma was and learned the love of such a beautiful animal that will be in my life forever.

One year after Demi came into my life, September 27, 1993, she died from complications of insulinoma surgery. I remember so vividly, even today, the day I took her in for her surgery. The day was gray and overcast and angel tears were falling from the sky. I remember the excruciating pain of losing my first little girl ferret. I still have a difficult time when I think about her—she taught me so much and changed my life in so many ways.

I miss you little angel girl.

Love,
Mommy
Virginia

If your ferret has insulinoma, make sure they eat frequently. Going without food for any length of time can cause your ferret to get extremely weak and possibly have a seizure. If you notice your ferret trembling or having difficult standing upright, rub a drop or two of Nutri-Cal or corn syrup on the ferret's gums to elevate the sugar level and quickly get them to eat something. You may have to supplement your ferret with one or two hand feedings per day. It is important for them to have small frequent meals, rather than one or two big ones. Follow up with a vet visit as soon as possible.

DIANA AND EPIMETHEUS

Dear God,
    Diana, one of our new girls, just stepped over the Rainbow Bridge today. She was a little princess named after The Princess; a pretty little petite dark sable girl who has now found peace in her life. She was dropped off with her cagemate at a pet store and left there to find a new home. Sadly, my Epimetheus had recently wandered away and so I took Diana home to live with us.
    God, if you see a little blaze boy with a snarl to his lip wandering around The Bridge, not knowing which direction to travel, please send the others over to get him. That would be my Epimetheus, wherever he is right now. He is just a little lost boy trying to find his way home. Tell him we love him very much and please give him his own stage and props because he sure liked to do a vaudeville show for us all. He loved to do the ferret dance of joy, too.
    Tell them all that their Mommy and Daddy love and miss everyone, even the ones we never really got to know well; they will always be in our hearts. The hope of seeing them all again at the Rainbow Bridge is the most wonderful thought we hold close to our hearts. My heart needs a lot of mending right now.

Donna and Dan
Wisconsin

P.S. Epimetheus "Eppy" was returned home many weeks later after being found and taken to the humane society where he was happily reunited with his family once again.

ELOISE

Eloise left us this afternoon after a brief bout with lymphosarcoma, which was diagnosed on Christmas Eve. She also had insulinoma and a right adrenal tumor, but those were slowing her down only about as much as being 7½ years old.

She was a sweet and happy girl up to the end. Yesterday she took a stroll across the floor to climb into her favorite box and bat two ping pong balls for a few minutes. Then she went in search of the crinkle sack to sleep in. Last night I put on soft music and held her for a long time; her breathing was becoming labored and she whimpered a little. She was also becoming incontinent, which upset her a lot. She was our only weasel who would tear through the house at 20 miles per hour to get to a litter pan. Today she was barely alert. I made sure she was comfortable with her lifelong friend sleeping beside her.

Eloise was one of our first two ferrets. She was never a cuddler, but she was the best kisser and probably the smartest ferret we have known. She climbed like a monkey, leapt like a flying squirrel and seemed to understand everything we wanted (or didn't want). She was a skinny little whippet with a pretty face and a love of life. When her sister's diabetes grew so bad she began to sleep all the time, Eloise stopped sleeping up on the third level of their cage and began to keep her sister company in the new bed on the bottom level. We were worried about how depressed Eloise would be when her sister died, but sadly, Eloise has gone first.

This evening we buried Eloise under the yellow rose bushes where she sleeps with the three old ladies we had adopted later on, and a brother who died earlier in the summer. St. Francis stands nearby to watch over them all.

Judith
Pennsylvania

I'm So Sleepy

A FUZZY'S PRAYER

Now I lay me down to sleep,
in my blankie, snuggled deep,
one more yawn to end the day,
tomorrow I will romp and play!
So God, if you could stay the night
to make sure I am covered tight,
tomorrow there's so much to do
before it's time to go with you.

My mommy taped up on the 'fridge
a poem about a special bridge.
I heard her cry again tonight,
so maybe you could hold her tight
until it's time for me to go.
My people here still need me so.
Oh, God, if only I could live,
I still have so much love to give.

- Liz Blackburn

ETHAN

I adopted Ethan in 1996, when he was between six months and one year old. The first thing he did when he came to live with us was to eat a tube of hand lotion. Ethan was an affectionate and gorgeous dark sable who enjoyed being a ferret and getting into mischief. He loved exploring, playing with his buddies, cuddling, being held and all the other things ferrets live for each day. He was outgoing but docile; you always knew he was around but he was never aggressive.

In May 2001, Ethan had surgery to remove a tumor. I received a call from the vet while he was on the operating table which is always a bad sign. It seemed that Ethan's tumor was so large and invasive, there was no chance of recovery even if he did make it through the surgery. The vet asked me what I wanted him to do. I made the very difficult decision to end his life while he was already under anesthesia. I did not want him to be in pain or have any more suffering; he was already 5 to 6 years old and in poor health. My heart was breaking once again. This year has been especially hard because I have lost several ferrets due to old age and disease within a short time.

I miss Ethan more than words can express. He was such an incredible ferret for the four years I knew him. I know he is now romping again happily with his buddies over the Rainbow Bridge.

I Love You Baby,
Mommy
Virginia

The better you know your ferret's habits, the easier it will be to detect a potential problem when they are not acting normal.

FATBOY SLIM

Over three years ago I learned of a ferret at the animal shelter. I couldn't sleep that night, and the next day I went to the shelter to see for myself. In the corner of the cage was the biggest, but skinniest, ferret I had ever seen. He looked so sad I wanted to cry, but didn't, I was just too mad. I took the poor boy to the front desk, paid the $50.00 fee and quickly took him home. I thought I was probably taking him home to die, but at least he would die in a comfortable home, not in a dark and cold cage. On the way home he licked me, bit me hard, and promptly went to sleep on my lap. We named him Slim Shady.

When we got home Slim started eating everything in sight—ferret food, dog food and whatever else he could get his teeth into. He never stopped eating and, within three months, we had to change his name to Fatboy Slim. He was huge, almost three times bigger than other full-grown ferrets. Sometimes he would lick my ankle several times and then bite down. I would look down, only to find him looking up at me with wide happy eyes. I couldn't get mad. He didn't know how to play and thought this was a funny game. I soon learned to pick my foot up as soon as I felt the first lick. He was gentle with the other "kids" and a loving father figure for the babies.

A few months ago Slim started getting slower and much fatter. The vet said Slim was very old and his heart didn't sound good. I knew his time was getting short. One day Slim's breathing became labored and, sadly, I knew the time had come to say goodbye. I fixed him a last meal of turkey baby food with broth and he licked up every last bit. I took him to the vet and held and loved him while he drifted off and away. God, please watch out for my big boy and please help him find his friends. I know they will be so glad to see him because he was a great snuggle buddy! Thank you, Slim, for the time you spent with us and the life lessons you taught us.

Mindy
Georgia

FRESNO

Fresno lost his battle with cancer today. Just two days ago he was romping with his friend, eating well and taking his medicine with a slight grimace. Yesterday he had a slow day, but I thought it was just a cold he'd been fighting off. Tonight I found him quivering but otherwise motionless; I had difficulty just trying to give him a little water. The emergency vet did what he could.

I realize in the grand scale of the universe, one tiny ferret's life may not matter so much. But Fresno touched my life in ways I can't even comprehend, making it a happier and more joyful place. He had a heart of gold and a spirit as bright as fire. Fresno, I'll always miss you.

I've had to get up four times while writing this, to grab the remaining ferret and take away the candy she's discovered. I guess I could move the candy bowl, but we both seem to need this right now. Life goes on, for some of us.

Fred
Colorado

 Learn the habits of all your fur-faced kids. Pay close attention to each one's habits so you will notice if one is lethargic, losing hair abnormally, coughing excessively, etc. This could mean there is a potential health problem. Have anything unusual checked out by a ferret-knowledgeable veterinarian.

FURRY

God, please welcome Furry to the Rainbow Bridge. He was our first ferret, and he crossed The Bridge on Sunday, August 5, 2001.

Furry had been through a lot—two adrenal gland surgeries, and the right adrenal gland tissue even grew back. He was bald and had just recently received a Lupron injection to help the symptoms. He also had to have his urethra rerouted a few months ago because he had a blockage from the prostate swelling, but he still kept fighting.

Furry's zest for life never left him. On Sunday morning he looked very bad, and I gave him some duck soup. He ate a small amount and ran around for five minutes. He wouldn't eat any more, so I put him back in with his friends, where he cuddled with them in the hammock for two hours. When I went to feed him at noon, he threw up what he had eaten earlier. His color was gray and he looked disoriented. We rushed him to the emergency vet, but by the time we arrived, Furry's stomach had swollen and he threw up again. We think he had developed an ulcer over a blood vessel. There was nothing we could have done to prevent what happened or treat it.

God, please direct him first to the tailor where he can get back the beautiful coat he once had. Also find him some jills[17] who would like a gentle and sweet lover. He was our first ferret and will always have a special place in our hearts. We will miss him.

Melody
New Jersey

---

[17] Female unaltered ferrets.

FUZZY

It has taken me a while to write this because it has been a very hard week. On March 4, 2002, my precious Fuzzy crossed over The Bridge. He has been with us for three years, and this month would have been about his fourth birthday.

Fuzzy has been such a joy to us. Almost every morning, while I am shaving, he would be there next to me, begging to be picked up so he could get a drink of water from the sink. He would then go to the kitchen and wait patiently in front of the refrigerator until I gave him a piece of cantaloupe. This was his favorite treat.

I can't get the picture of him out of my mind; thinking of him during our time at the vet's office, before we had to help him to The Bridge. I will always think there must have been something else I could have done.

We will always miss you,
Michael and Violeta
Colorado

 Be careful of little feet under rocking chairs. If you are sitting in the rocking chair, your ferret will probably be right there with you, begging for attention.

GODIVA

God, could you please look for a little one named Godiva? She came into our shelter quite a while ago and was the first formal adoption. Due to adrenal disease, she was completely bald except for her beautiful little face. We named her Lady Godiva.

She had adrenal surgery and grew back a beautiful new coat. We thought her new coat would be sable in color but it grew back light and very softly colored.

Someone adopted Godiva and then moved away from our area. One day we received an e-mail letting us know Godiva had a second adrenal surgery and, unfortunately, did not make it through this time.

Please tell Lady Godiva she was much loved by many people and she is missed. Also, please give her kisses from all of us she left behind.

Linda and Karen
North Carolina

Cotton swabs can be used to clean ferret ears. Dip the swab into some comfortably warm water and shake the excess water off the swab before inserting it into the ear. This way, the swab is slightly damp and warm. Clean the outer ear area but do not go deeply into the ear canal. Next, take a dry swab and wipe the ear again to make sure it is completely dry. Use as many swabs as necessary until there is no ear wax on the swab. For very dirty ears, use a gentle ear cleanser such as Oti-Clens® (available at the pet store) or Vet Solutions Ear Cleanser® (available at your vet). Avoid using alcohol or hydrogen peroxide for cleaning ears because they are very drying and irritating to tender ferret ear tissue.

GONZO

God, I just wanted to write a quick note to you. This is Julie in Savannah, and I lost another longtime friend at 5:00 this morning. Gonzo had been really sick and I noticed his brother giving him extra special attention last night. I got him out of the cage and started to snuggle him. I laid him in the bed with me because I wanted to watch over him closely during the night.

When I woke up just before 5:00 o'clock, I said a prayer:

> "Please, Lord, take this frail weak body and make him full again. Let him play in the sunshine, and let him have fun with his friends. He will be missed terribly. Amen."

I let his brother see him after he died. When he started licking him, I started to cry. He will miss his brother so much and so will his mommy. Please God, help him find the family ferrets that went before him. Gonzo will be coming with his favorite blankie and ball. He will probably be hungry and thirsty because he refused to eat. Please tell him I love him and I will be there to get him shortly. Let him know that his brother is fine. Mommy loves you, monkey boy. Be free, have fun, and enjoy your new life.

Love, Mommy
Georgia

Ferrets tire of cold hard crunchy food day after day. For a treat, put some of their regular crunchy food in a dish and cover it with warm water. Mix this around to make a little "gravy." Make sure it is not too hot. Call everybody to dinner and watch them eat this up like crazy. They will drink the water out of the dish first, so be prepared to add more warm water as needed. Yummy!

GYPSY

Dear God,

My first baby, Gypsy, passed over the Rainbow Bridge yesterday and I'd really appreciate it if you could welcome her in. She's a tiny sable girl, very sweet and playful. She loves to tumble in the grass with other fuzzies. She leaves behind her sister and brother. We all miss her, but I know she's in a better place with you. There's no more pain or discomfort. Please remind her that we love her and someday we will all meet again.

Sherri
Massachusetts

If your ferrets are free roaming most of the time, keep them in a confined and secure area for their safety when you are not at home or sleeping. As hard as you try to make a house ferret-proof, ferrets are very curious by nature and can find things to get into, under and behind that you don't even know about. Also, if you had an emergency and had to evacuate quickly, there would not be enough time to search the house to find them. If they are secure in a small room or cage, you could get gather them up quickly enough and out of the house to safety. Prepare in advance for emergencies and always have a plan of action for all your furry critters.

HANDSOME

There is a very special ferret named Handsome that needs to be welcomed to the Rainbow Bridge, shown around and helped to find his friend who is already there. He loves stuffed toys, the girl ferrets and needs a good meal because he's eaten very little lately.

We had the special luck to care for Handsome for the past ten months. When he came to our house, he was a big boy of 4½ pounds and overjoyed with his new home. He had been a shelter ferret who was not given the love, care, attention or herbal supplement he needed. He was diagnosed over three years ago with cardiomyopathy and was given no more than six months to live at the time. But Handsome defied all odds.

He loved following the girl ferrets around, dooking all the while. He adored stuffed animals, the bigger the better, which he hid under the couch or in his hammock. Handsome was so full of life and would play forever with toys he grasped in his large paws. When he tried to jump over obstacles, he would usually land on his belly, pretending it didn't happen as if embarrassed to have anyone see him like this. He made us laugh and filled our house with joy.

Handsome's health problems and age finally caught up with him recently and we had to make the painful decision to have him helped out of his suffering. Our hearts are heavy and tears are shed for you tonight, Handsome. Our lives are much richer for having you share our house and love. You will be missed, goodbye Handsome.

Linda
Kansas

HEIDI

I was so proud of the ferret I adopted two weeks ago named Heidi; I nicknamed her Hideykins. She loved to hide under the covers and had a fetish for chewing leather. Heidi quit eating and drinking last Sunday for some unknown reason. I handfed her all week and took her to the vet every day for fluids. She did well Friday evening but didn't make it through the night. She was so tiny she didn't have any reserves to fall back on.

A necropsy revealed an enlarged liver, pancreatitis and an inflamed stomach with ulcers. The vet concluded her condition was due to a poor diet compounded by her small size. There was nothing anyone could have done to help Heidi by the time she was surrendered to our shelter.

It has been a hard week. I had Heidi such a short time. I will always remember her licking my face, chasing a golf ball all around the apartment and having her curled up fast asleep on my chest. She was a perfect ferret and I know she waits for me at the front door of my heavenly home.

Oklahoma

Sometimes younger ferrets will pick on the older and weaker ferrets, dragging them around by the scruff of the neck. Since the older ones are not as strong any more, they are unable to defend themselves. If a not-so-old ferret gets dragged around by another ferret, this could be a sign of sickness or weakness that you may not be aware of. Like other animals, ferrets always know when one of them is in a weakened condition.

HERMES

Dear God,

    Well, it happened tonight. I can't say that I am shocked by this because I've seen it coming for two months now. But, I didn't expect the way it came. Hermes' companion passed away two months ago. When we got them, they were very attached to each other and wouldn't get along with other ferrets. We worked vigilantly to fatten them up, get them healthy and get rid of their intestinal worms. They were daddy's boys and followed him around all the time. When the brother passed away, we were very worried about Hermes and now I am saying goodbye again.

    Hermes had been moping around, not eating well and tolerating my insistence that he eat. After his brother died, Hermes missed him so much that he never did hop and pop and have fun like he used to. This morning I found a black tarry stool and we ran him to the vet. The vet said it was blood and felt a ping-pong ball-sized mass in his belly. After testing, it was felt the mass was inoperable cancer. Even if we considered surgery, Hermes probably wouldn't have been strong enough to endure it.

    We brought Hermes home and made the appointment to have him euthanized the next day. However, he didn't want to wait that long. He began convulsing, clicking his teeth, drooling and refused to eat or drink. We rushed him to the emergency vet and helped him cross the Rainbow Bridge. I had selfishly made the appointment for the next day hoping against hope that he would perk up and all would be well. I really wasn't prepared to let him go. His daddy has taken this pretty hard. Hermes was his boy; I was just lucky to get in the way of a kiss from time to time.

    Another star shines brightly tonight because it was just added to the heavens. Hermes is now with his brother once again. I'm sure they are chasing each other through tubes like they used to do; Hermes thumping his big fluffy tail back and forth against the tube. I know there is one big dooking party going on at The Bridge tonight. There has to be because the biggest, most beautiful caramel colored ferret with huge feet and a huge fluffy tail just arrived.

When a boy that beautiful shows up, there has to be a party. Mom and Dad miss them both and feel really sad right now, but we know they are together again.

April and Damon
Florida

 Being without electricity recently late one night at feeding time for the older ferrets, I was unable to heat up the frozen food cubes in the microwave or on the electric stove. Since this is all some of the ferrets eat each morning and at night, I was a little worried. Then I remembered I had cans of Hill's a/d Prescription Diet food in the cupboard. Usually, I mix the food with a little water and warm it in the microwave, but tonight they got it at room temperature. Pick up several cans of Hill's a/d canine/feline food (there is no "ferret" variety) from your vet or chicken baby food from the grocery store to have on hand. Buy whatever they will eat best for those on blended ferret food like "duck soup"[18] or other homemade recipes. This could be helpful in case of emergencies such as being without electricity or running out of their normal ferret food.

---

[18] There are several variations of the "duck soup" recipe found on the Internet. I don't know why it is called "duck soup" because there are no ducks in it and I personally don't know any ducks that eat soup. It is usually a mixture of chicken baby food, dry ferret food and a few other ingredients mixed in a blender. It is used for sick, aging or recovering ferrets.

HOUDINI

It's been about a month since I had to say goodbye to my first ferret. He had adrenal gland disease. We were treating it, but it got so bad. God, please take care of my little love bug, Houdini. I hope he's all furry and playful like he was when he was younger.

He was my first baby and we had him cremated. When I got him about five years ago, he was a flying bundle of teeth and fur. He quickly learned to escape from three of his cages, thus the name Houdini. Shortly thereafter, he turned into quite a snuggler.

I sent his remains to a nice lady who paints portraits of animals on eggshells and then fills them with their remains.[19] I'll be getting my egg back tomorrow.

Thanks, God, for taking such good care of my baby.

Erin
Minnesota

 When opening an outside door, always look down at your feet to see which furry "kid" wants to go out for a walk. Make sure no one in the family opens the door without checking first so no little fuzzy feet escape outdoors. Even rattling your keys will get the snuggle bunnies heading toward the door from a sound sleep. Unfortunately, ferrets will explore the great outdoors and not know how to get back home. This could end in tragedy very quickly. If you take your ferret outside, always use a ferret harness and leash to avoid any escapes.

---

[19] Find the website address for The Eggcellent Collection in the appendix.

HUBERT

Please, God, check on Hubert for me. He had liver cancer and crossed The Bridge suddenly yesterday. I grieve so for him. He left this world in my arms with my lipstick on his nose. The vet said it was the kindest thing I could have done. I know he lived a long life, but I miss him.

Catherine
Utah

If your fuzzbunnies stop eating or drinking, hand feed them and give them water from a paper cup. If this doesn't work, get a small plastic syringe from the drug store or your vet. Hold the head gently and put small amounts of water or food into the side of the mouth very slowly. Give them plenty of time to swallow so they do not inhale the food or water.

HUMPHREY

We had to help Humphrey cross over The Bridge on Saturday. I will miss his large warm brown eyes and rich chocolate fur.

God, please help him find his friends and make sure he gets all the sweet treats he wants.

The Humpinator is terribly missed here; we are so sad. We love you Humpy. Even though we had him only a year and a half after adopting him from a shelter, he brightened our lives.

June
Kentucky

Ferrets, while generally quiet, can make a variety of noises. The chuckle or chatter sound they make when happy or excited is generally referred to as "dooking." When frightened or cornered, they make an "inside out" hissing noise. It's the kind of sound you make if you suck in your breath through your lips. Ferrets can whimper, cry, squeal, cough, sneeze, hiccup, scream and some even bark. Learn the sounds your ferret makes so you know when they are happy or in distress.

JB

JB finally succumbed to a long battle with insulinoma yesterday evening. JB was born on November 26, 1995. We heard about him at a ferret show in December but he was still a kit and too young to be separated from his mother. We waited until March the next year and drove from Massachusetts to Maryland to see him.

What we found was a great big muscle-bound athlete decked out with a beautiful sable outfit, complete with white ascot and a pedigree that goes back further than anyone we ever knew. He was named John Bear Fertipton Ferret, after the old Millionaire television show, and he was promptly dubbed JB.

We soon discovered that JB was a bit of a coward and was compensating by overreacting to the smallest of inconveniences. He also was developing the hormones of a teenager. Our home was threatened when he pushed a 20-pound antique lamp off of a table and broke it. Thank goodness for super glue. Also there was the small matter of a scent which announced to all that a ferret lived here. JB was absolutely terrified of bathtubs. A kitchen sink was acceptable for a bath, but he became a raging monster in the tub.

We gave him lots of love and after he was neutered at seven months, we all settled into a routine that caused the days and years to pass too quickly. JB mellowed and learned to stay quiet in my jacket on morning walks. He became a special ambassador for all ferrets and participated in several public educational events.

A year ago, during his annual exam, a blood test unexpectedly showed low blood sugar. He had surgery and was put on Prednisone[20]. He was just fine for about a year, but suddenly started refusing his medication a few weeks ago. Sometimes we could trick him into taking it and he also started occasionally refusing food as well. JB had lots of spunk and I do miss him an awful lot.

William
Massachusetts

---

[20] See the appendix for a description of this medication.

JASMINE

Jasmine, our 4-year-old dark-eyed white ferret, died last night of post-operative complications. She stopped breathing shortly after midnight on June 18, 1999.

Jasmine joined our family as a 4-month-old kit. Jasmine helped our three other ferrets become integrated as a family. Since she was still a kit, she was accepted fairly quickly. Jasmine was full of energy and loved to crawl under the cage carpet, knocking over all the food bowls in the process. She could dig in the litter box until it was nearly empty. She loved to climb on furniture, and scaled a bookcase to reach the top of a file cabinet where ferret supplies were kept. Jasmine was the first to discover how to pry open the connecting tube between the two cages and let everyone escape. Once we came home and found apples and potting soil all over the kitchen floor and five ferrets merrily exploring the house. Jasmine loved squeaky toys, especially dog toys that she would hide under the couch.

Jasmine was a beautiful silvery ferret as a kit. As she got older, she lost most of the darker hairs and became almost white. People often commented on how pretty she was. Jasmine had a very easy-going and sweet disposition. She got along with everyone and seemed oblivious to the dominance struggles of some of the other ferrets. A couple of years ago, Jasmine's coat started to show signs of adrenal disease. Since she didn't act sick and a thick coat of fur returned, we didn't have surgery at the time. She was, however, overeating and getting fat. We were used to sick ferrets refusing to eat and losing weight. When antibiotics didn't have any effect on her enlarged spleen, we began to think seriously about surgery.

She began acting very sick, not playing anymore and acting uncomfortable, so we decided to schedule surgery. We expected the surgery to be a routine spleen and adrenal tumor removal. Much to our surprise, a huge right adrenal tumor was blocking blood flow and ready to rupture.

After surgery, we took Jasmine home and she had a rough night. We went back to the vet in the morning and she was given fluids and an injection. She slept comfortably for a long time and we thought she was improving. At night she became restless again. It looked like she would have another rough night. Her tail was puffed, in retrospect a bad sign. We brought the hospital cage upstairs again so she could sleep right next to our bed. Soon after we turned out the lights, we heard several high-pitched cries. We turned on the lights and sat next to her. She cried two or three more times and stopped breathing. Ironically, there was only one other time a ferret of ours faced a difficult surgical recovery. Jasmine was the young and healthy blood donor who saved one of our other ferret's lives.

Jasmine will be buried next to our dog at a beautiful pet cemetery in a rural area of Maryland. Her picture will be on her little tombstone so everyone will know she was a ferret, a ferret who was loved. Goodbye Jazzy; we'll never forget you. Four years was much too short.

Clare and Bill
Maryland

A critical time for your ferret is three to four weeks after adrenal surgery, especially if both adrenal glands have been removed. Watch to see that they are eating normally and do not go without food for any length of time. Your ferret needs a hormone replacement injection (Percorten[21]) to enable the body to compensate for the loss of the adrenal glands. Without this, your ferret can crash which can quickly become a life-threatening situation. Consult with your ferret's veterinarian.

---

[21] See the appendix for a description of this medication.

JASMINE

We lost our little old lady, Jasmine, today. She would have been 8 years old in April 2002. She was diagnosed with adrenal disease back in September 2001 and then we noticed she was having hind leg weakness. Back to the vet we went for blood work. She was diagnosed with insulinoma. Both the vet and we decided that surgery was not an option for her because of her age. My husband and I discussed at length what to do, deciding that we would make the best of whatever time she had left with us and make her as comfortable as possible. I guess her tired old body decided it couldn't fight it anymore and gave up. She died quietly in her sleep, curled up in her hammock. I found her late this afternoon when it was time to give her some out time.

Jasmine is not the first ferret I have lost, but she has hit me the hardest. I have been in tears since I found her. My husband and I knew that her time on this earth was somewhat limited, but just thought, or rather hoped that the time would be longer than it was. God, I miss her so much already. She was our cranky old lady, did not like to be held, but was getting better at it since I had been giving her "duck soup." She would curl up in my arms and slurp her duck soup like it was the greatest.

I know in my heart that she is in a much better place and more at peace with herself and has hopefully found her one true love, Baby, who we lost almost three years ago.

Rest in peace pretty girl, mommy loves you and misses you.

Massachusetts

Use a bungee cord to hold the litter box in place in your ferret's cage. If the litter box is left unsecured, it will make a fun game for your ferrets to see who can tip it over first. Be sure to remove the tiny rubber tips at each end of the bungee cord and dispose of them so they are not eaten.

JASMINE

Today I lost my best friend. I was lucky enough to share almost six years with her. Jasmine was a special lady whose big heart and warrior spirit always amazed me. From the second our eyes were drawn to each other, I knew we would be together. Apparently, so did she, because she climbed up my arm and settled herself on my shoulder. She spent many hours on my shoulder as I did chores around the house. This is not easy with a ferret supervising.

She loved socks and was a thief extraordinaire but, even more than the socks; she loved the chase to get them back. Most of the time she would get them to safety in her hidey hole where I couldn't reach them. She would then come out looking very smug. She had her troll doll babies and her pacifier collection she garnered from my grandson. She arranged these every day, counted and guarded them from all sneak attacks. She had a fondness for ferret vitamins and an occasional cranberry raisin. She cleaned everyone's ears, they were all dirty, you see. She was the alpha ferret and made sure the others knew that. Nobody ever argued the point. She taught many children the value of love and kindness. She taught me so many things and I will miss her yawns in the morning, her nose touches on my ankle, her shoulder sitting and her gentle nose kisses. She enjoyed rearranging the dirt and grass snorkeling.

Jasmine and I had many adventures, some sadness and a lot of laughter. She's been through many trials but, ever the warrior, came through it all. I guess I knew she always would.

Today my heart aches because my friend has moved on. I have lost a special part of my life. Shine down little star, yours is one of the brightest. You'll always be in my heart.

Sandy
New Mexico

JASPER

Saturday Jasper was fine, bouncing around and acting normal. Sunday morning he seemed a little depressed, but no big red flags went off for us. Since Jasper was in the early stages of insulinoma, having a sleepy morning was not necessarily out of the ordinary for him. Although I had to work on Sunday, I came home for lunch and found him hiding under a bed. When I scooped him up, I noticed his belly was extremely bloated and hard. Our local vet was out of town, so we rushed forty-five minutes to the next town for emergency surgery. I did not know the vet, but we had no other options available at the time. I was in the room for the surgery, which went smoothly. The doctor removed a hairball mass from Jasper's intestine and a small piece of black rubber material from his stomach.

After the surgery, the vet said we could take Jasper home. I was concerned about leaving so soon because Jasper was barely coming out of the anesthetic. Reluctantly, we loaded up and headed for home. He seemed to be doing fine at first, squirming a bit, but generally sleeping. After about three hours, I noticed his jaws were really clenched tight and a slight rasp to his breathing. I decided to call the vet anyway to see what he thought. His suggestion was that Jasper might be a little cold. He also said that given Jasper's age (6 years old), he would take some time to come out of the anesthetic. We had been through adrenal surgery with Jasper about a year ago and did know the importance of keeping him warm. Figuring the vet should know what he was talking about, we relaxed a bit and warmed up a heating pad for Jasper.

Less than an hour later, I was sitting next to Jasper and he coughed once. I scooped him up, figuring he was probably waking up. He suddenly coughed a few more times, squeaked loudly and he was gone. Our world shattered! I was so sure that Jasper was going to pull through this and be fine. The vet even checked things out during the surgery and said he could see no problems with the pancreas. Obviously, his insulinoma was not progressing very rapidly and his other organs appeared to be in good shape.

We lost our only other ferret just eight months ago to lymphoma. I guess we did not realize how much Jasper helped us get through that difficult time until he was gone. When our first ferret died, Jasper was always there for kisses and cuddles and it really seemed to help us deal with our grief. Now we are totally alone and having an incredibly hard time dealing with it. Our apartment seems so quiet and lonely without our little "dookers" running around.

Brett and Melissa
Montana

Good things to have on hand at all times in case of illness:
- ♥ *Pedialyte (water with electrolytes used for dehydration)*
- ♥ *Chicken baby food (most ferrets will eat this even when sick)*
- ♥ *Hill's canned a/d Prescription Diet (they love this)*
- ♥ *Small paper cups (they love to drink out of cups)*
- ♥ *Plastic spoons (these feel better on their mouths than metal ones)*
- ♥ *Pill splitter for medications (purchase at a drug store)*
- ♥ *Ferritone (vitamin supplement that ferret's love)*
- ♥ *Nutri-Cal (ferret variety found at the pet store) or corn syrup*

JASPER

Jasper had bilateral adrenal surgery and was not doing well. He was at the hospital for several days receiving subcutaneous fluids. When I saw him on Saturday, he did not look good, but we were still hopeful. When I called to check on him on Monday, the doctor said he wanted to talk to me. I knew it was bad. Jasper was not improving and I made that heartbreaking decision to not let him suffer anymore.

I brought him home so he could see his home once again and to say goodbye to his buddies. When he first got home, he actually had a bit of pep in him and got into some mischief in the living room. We took some pictures of him and, in some of them, you can see the old Jasper looking out. When it was time to return to the hospital, you could see in his face how tired he was and how much his little body wanted to rest. I put him on his snuggle sack and got some pictures of his buddies saying goodbye. During the car ride, he sat in his sack with his head sticking out; he was calm and quiet. Jasper was always such a good boy. I told him how much I loved him and how sorry I was.

I gave him a few Cheerios when we got to the hospital. He took his last lick of vitamins and was gone. It was very peaceful.

I love all my fuzzies, but Jasper went a little deeper in my heart. You hate to admit it, but sometimes one of them touches you more. I think during the last month, especially with the feedings, vet visits and such, it brought me even closer. He wasn't even 3 years old. I am having him cremated and bought a little urn with a ferret figurine on it. That way he will always be with me. I told my significant other that if I died before him, I want all the little urns buried with me.

Amy
New York

JEREMY

I adopted Jeremy in January 1997. He fit in well with the other ferrets in the household and was a very gentle soul. In 1999, he had one of his adrenal glands and his spleen removed and recovered fully within a few weeks. He was a cuddler and always loved to snuggle close to his buddies.

One summer I decided to pack up all the ferrets for a road trip to see my daughter and several other family members who lived about seven hours away from me. This was the first trip I had made since living with ferrets for many years. I thought I could manage the planned five-day visit even though there were special feedings, medications, and older ferrets whose routine and comfort I did not want to upset. I bought two large cages and, along with a smaller cage to house one of the older boys, packed and secured everything in my van for the long drive. I knew it was going to be a challenge because the ferrets were free-roaming and not used to being confined in a cage. I wasn't sure how they would react, especially while being jostled around in a moving vehicle. We all arrived at my daughter's home several hours later and ready for a new adventure for the next few days.

The next morning, I took Jeremy out of the cage and brought him into the kitchen while I fixed his breakfast. We were the only two up this early and the house was quiet. I no sooner placed him on the kitchen floor and he was already disappearing into a small hole under the kitchen cabinet. The only thing I could see was the tip of his tail. It happened so fast, I was unable grab him to prevent him from going into the hole. I quickly realized what a big mistake I had made to even let him in the kitchen without first making sure the room was ferret-proofed. I began to panic and wonder how I could get him out and, what would happen if he didn't come out on his own. I had visions of the kitchen being torn apart and destroyed just to get Jeremy out. I considered that there could be another hole to the outside of the house where he could escape even further out of my reach. I got down on my hands and knees to see if I had any way of reaching him. The hole was so small I was unable to get my fingers inside, let alone my whole hand. I was amazed that Jeremy had somehow managed to get himself inside such a small hole in a split second because he was quite a large ferret. While down on the floor, I called him and made a "kissing" noise that the ferrets usually respond to. Luckily, he poked his head out of the hole to see if he was going to get fed. He then proceeded to get his body out far enough so I could grab him and pull him the rest of the way out. I felt very fortunate at that moment. A tragedy had been prevented and possibly his life had been saved that day. Jeremy remained in his cage with the rest of the ferrets for the remainder of our visit.

To this day, I have not told my daughter about this incident and how her kitchen was saved from destruction. She is not fond of ferrets anyway, would not have wanted Jeremy in the kitchen, and certainly would have been upset if I had begun to smash the kitchen cabinets with a hammer and a crowbar.

In May 2001, Jeremy had exploratory surgery because x-rays showed air pockets in his chest cavity and abdomen. Once in surgery, the doctor found Jeremy had insulinoma and many cancerous tumors. Jeremy was approximately 5 to 6 years old, not a strong ferret at the time, and he did not survive the surgery. I was devastated because I had just lost another ferret the previous day in surgery. Losing two ferrets, especially in the same week, is more than anyone should have to bear. He was also the fifth ferret I lost within five months.

I will always remember with great fondness what a gentle and loving ferret Jeremy was in the four years I knew him. He enriched my life beyond measure.

> I miss you baby,
> Love, Mom
> Virginia

JESSE

At 10:10 this morning, I had to help Jesse cross the Rainbow Bridge. I could never have imagined anything more heartbreaking. He had been sick a long time. The Prednisone he had been taking didn't help much, and then last night he started going downhill. He started choking and having difficulty breathing. I didn't want him to die like that.

God, will you please see that he finds everything he needs. He loved sweets, although he rarely got any. He loved anything rubbery; I guess he didn't know those things could be harmful to him. He loved sleeping in big comfy comforters. Please tell him we love him so much and Mommy is sorry he had to go. He will always have a place in our hearts.

Corynne and Joel
Seattle

Observe your ferrets' play habits to make sure none of them chew electrical cords or curly phone cords. Usually they don't attempt it, but I've heard of a few that did. Enclose electrical cords in a plastic sleeve like those used for straightening up those messy computer cables behind the PC. The plastic sleeves are available from hardware and home improvement centers. For a less expensive solution, get an empty carpet tube, cut it down to size, and cut a slit down the entire length for stuffing cords inside. Keep hanging phone cords out of reach so no one gets tangled in them or chews on them.

Let Me Out Please

BLESSINGS

A fuzzy kiss to start the day
means more than words can ever say,
Fuzzy whispers in my ear,
little whiskers, soft and dear.

A little shadow follows me,
a little nudge . . . what can it be?
Just my fuzzy at my feet,
innocent and looking sweet.

A little furball on the run,
life so brief, but so much fun!
Misplaced poopies on the rug,
trusting eyes, a fuzzy hug.

Bedtime when I tuck you in,
a goodnight kiss, a tickled chin.
Special blessings all day long,
I'll miss them so when you are gone.

So now I treasure every one
until your little life is done.
'Cuz in our house we know it's true;
our home is blessed because of you.

- Liz Blackburn

JEWEL

Yesterday I lost my little girl, Jewel; she was 5 years old. Jewel had been sick on and off for about six months and had been taking Lupron for her adrenal tumor. Last week, I packed up the four ferrets and went to visit my mom. While visiting, I noticed Jewel was getting very weak and began drinking an excessive amount of water. I found a vet that treated ferrets and took her in. After some tests were run, I found out that Jewel had diabetes. The doctor wanted her to stay at the hospital while he started her on insulin.

I went to visit Jewel twice a day in the hospital to cuddle and feed her. I told her how much I loved and missed her. When I visited on Friday morning, she appeared to be getting better and I told her she would be coming home on Saturday. Unfortunately, last night I got that horrible phone call from the vet that said she didn't make it. I have been crying ever since. Even my ferrets seem to be very depressed and my little boy slept all night on the pocketbook Jewel used to carry around the house.

This morning I buried my little mush girl, Jewel, in my mom's garden. We planted a beautiful lavender bush and some purple flowers around her, and then we said goodbye.

My Jewel was the sweetest, cutest and most loveable little ferret who was the "whipped cream queen." She loved to drink out of plastic cups and then run away with them to hide them under my bed. She would carry my makeup bag around the house after she had removed all the contents just so she could store her treats in it. She would lie next to me when I was sitting on the floor watching TV and roll over so I would rub her belly. I miss her sitting on my feet begging for treats while I'm working on the computer. Jewel, you will be missed dearly.

Iris
New York

JUNIOR

God, please look out for a cute little panda ferret named Junior. Please make sure he finds his way and feels safe and loved. Also, please tell him his Mom still cries for him and smiles when thinking of him everyday. His brother, Fatboy Slim[22], took his departure hard, as we all did. Slim now has a new fur buddy. Tell our June Bug that by no means has this new boy taken his place; no one ever will. We know they would have loved each other and played together. The new guy has heard many Junior stories and has many more to hear.

One more thing, God—my horse, Ollie, also passed over The Bridge recently. Ollie was very sweet and loved the smell of ferrets. Maybe if he and Junior could meet up there, they could look out for each other until I join them. It would make me feel a lot better. Thank you for all your help.

Mindy
Georgia

 Look for lumps in throw rugs around the house; it could be a ferret sleeping contently and soundly. Never step on a lumpy rug. Instead, pick up the rug and look underneath it for that fuzzy critter.

---

[22] See Fatboy Slim's story elsewhere in the book.

KARI

Kari died this week. It was not much of a surprise because her lymphoma was terminal, but it is the latest in a string of losses which really hits hard. Last summer we had six ferrets and now we have two. We think Kari was 4 to 5 years old. Now all our little girls have left us, leaving the last two ferrets to huddle together in a small ferret heap. Kari was met at The Bridge by the four that are already there.

For so long, six seemed like the right number of ferrets to care for; now two in the cage seem so lonely. My five human kids miss them all, too.

Jean
Michigan

Cover the ferret cage with a blanket or towels because ferrets enjoy sleeping in the darkness. You might even have to wake them up at playtime because they will sleep longer with a blanket covering the cage.

KASPER

Dear God,
 This is Buffie. I'm the one that asked for the prayer when one of my ferrets was sick. He passed away in my arms on November 6, 2001, at 1:00 A.M., and I was so upset.
 I've had pets all my life and, of course, I cried when they passed away but got over it in a short time. It's been two months now since I lost my first fuzzy. His name was Kasper and I haven't gotten over it yet. I am still crying because I miss him so much. It hurts so bad I don't think I will ever get over it. A few months ago I took a video of all my ferrets playing, and I cry when I see Kasper. My other ferrets took the loss pretty well.
 God, can you please tell me how to cope? How long does it take to get over such a loss and move on?

> I love you very much,
> Buffie
> Texas

If you have a dedicated ferret room, try covering the window (either all or half) with some clear cling film to diffuse the light. Although ferrets prefer sleeping in darkness, they need to have the benefits of sunlight just like we do. You don't want to leave the room in darkness with the blinds drawn all day while you are at work, nor do you want the sunlight heating up the room too much during hot summer afternoons.

KATIE

Dear God,
 Please watch out for Katie, she's just two weeks shy of her first birthday. She'll be the little chocolate girl who will stand up and dance for Savory Nuggets. She has the most beautiful eyes and blinks a lot. I'm sure she'll appreciate the fresh air now that her lungs work. You may have trouble finding her since she never got in trouble, but check the cabinets and the cool wood floor where she liked to lay flat. And please find her a security cube, she's bright and sunny but gets nervous if she can't sleep in the dark. Tell her Mommy and Daddy love her. Also tell her that there are already two other ferrets she never met already up there who can help her out. Thanks.

New Jersey

Recycle the metal rabies tags your vet gives you when the ferrets have their rabies shots—use them as colorful Christmas tree decorations. They come in shiny red, green, blue, gold and orange and are shaped like bells, ovals and hearts. Since they have a small hole in the top already, use a metal ornament hanger or a piece of string to attach it to the tree. The tags work best on small or tabletop trees.

KIRBY

Unlike many of the other ferrets in the household, you'd never know Kirby was around. He was always in the background and was not aggressive like some of the others.

Kirby was a beautiful sable boy who I adopted in April 1997. It was thought at the time he was somewhere between 2 and 3 years old. He fit in with all the other ferrets right from the start, and sometimes that's a tough task. Usually, there are twelve to fifteen ferrets living here and at one time, there were nineteen ferrets and two cats. It's not always easy for a new ferret to live harmoniously with the others. Some of the ferrets have taken as long as one year before they were accepted by the others. Not Kirby. He was sweet, quiet and cuddly; the others liked to snuggle up with him to nap.

Kirby loved to eat Cheerios and would always show up when he heard the squeaky toy that I used to let them know when it was treat time.

He was not in good health for the past couple of years and last year it was determined that he had so many problems that surgery was not an option for him. He had insulinoma and probably adrenal disease as well, skin tumors, urinary blockage, anemia, etc. What was the hardest for me to see was the way his abdomen bloated up because of his blockage. It was difficult for him to urinate so he would wait as long as he could which then made a huge puddle when he finally let go. He was uncomfortable and had difficulty walking around because of the weight of his huge abdomen. He could not even tuck his feet together in a tight circle like ferrets love to do or get his foot up to give himself a good scratching. His body was so large his little legs looked like skinny little chicken legs. But how I loved those little chicken legs and I tried my best to help him get around whenever I could, picking him up and moving him from room to room so he could continue to socialize and play when he felt up to it.

For well over one year he would not eat crunchy food out of the dish, but looked forward with anticipation to eating the blended

Fuzzbean Crossing

and warmed food I gave him each morning and night. He was on a daily dosage of Prednisone also.

Kirby surprised me by hanging on for as long as he did. I was prepared, as much as you can be for any loss, to have him leave long before the end of last year and he certainly surpassed that. So one day recently, when he showed no interest in eating, it did not come as a total surprise—it was finally his time to leave. He had stayed with us much longer than I ever thought he would.

On February 6, 2001, and somewhere around 7 years old, Kirby slipped away to cross the Rainbow Bridge. He had always been a very sweet and gentle soul, and I loved having him in my life for almost four years. His body is finally at peace and he will be greatly missed.

Mommy
Virginia

Always do a "nose" count when leaving the house or retiring for the night. That way, you can rest easy knowing that all the fuzzy ones are safe and sound in their room or cage.

KOALA

We've been preparing for some time for the loss of our first ferret—a blind 8 year old with insulinoma—but it was another ferret, Koala, who brought us to the emergency clinic. X-rays revealed extensive pulmonary edema on one side which made the vet suspect trauma. There had been no trauma we could think of. Blood tests revealed that she was also fighting a serious infection. She made it through the night on oxygen and antibiotics.

During a visit to the doctor the following day, Koala collapsed and died. She was only 4 years old. It was such a shock because we thought she'd outlive all the others.

God, please watch for Koala, a petite dark sable. She doesn't have anyone to meet her from our house, but she's cheery and outgoing. She will easily make friends to hang out with while she waits for the rest of her family to join her there.

Nancy
Minnesota

Be careful when grabbing your ferret quickly. If your ferret has an enlarged spleen, it could be ruptured by grabbing around the lower body. One way to tell if the spleen is enlarged is to notice if the abdomen is enlarged. Stand above the ferret and look down the length of the body. If it looks pear shaped and the abdomen is extended, have this condition checked by your vet. It could possibly be an enlarged spleen.

KUMA

Dear God,

It is with great sadness I ask you to watch for Kuma, my little bear ferret. He's had a rough life, but I hope during the last few months we made up for the bad times he had before we knew him. Please tell him how much we love and miss him.

Kuma is a funny old dark sable guy who loves vitamins and just learned what it is to dook and dance last month. Over the last few days his little body began shutting down. He passed away this afternoon, snuggled with my kitty in his hammock.

I also have a special request, God—Kuma never lived with another ferret and was a bit afraid of them. He loved my dogs and cats, though, and always dooked and danced with them like crazy. If you could please arrange it so my dog and cat angels could visit him, it would make us both feel better. Thank you God.

Amanda
Michigan

Riddle: Why do ferrets sleep so much?

Answer: To give you a chance to rest and recuperate before they wake up and wear you to a frazzle.

KYLE

At approximately 12:18 A.M. on June 7, 2002, my dear sweet baby Kyle was helped to The Bridge. Kyle had suffered from insulinoma for about a year and a half and was just diagnosed with adrenal disease last month. Kyle was met at the Bridge by his two brothers and his loving little sister. Kyle would have been 7 years old in October this year. My fiancé is taking it especially hard, as Kyle was always a daddy's boy.

God, watch out when Kyle gets there. He is as wild as the thunderstorm we had here in Baltimore tonight. Batten down the hatches and hide your socks.

Goodnight my Kyle bunny. I love you forever and miss you with all my heart.

Aileen
Maryland

Keep those fuzzbunnies cool in the hot weather by keeping the air conditioner running and don't take them outdoors for any length of time when the temperature is above 80°. Most importantly, do not leave the ferrets in a carrier in the hot car while you run a quick errand.

LITTLE FANG

Little Fang came to us at three months old, as a gift to my son. Within days we were stricken to the very bone with this thing called "ferret love." He was now a member of our family, and we loved him unconditionally.

Fang chose his family position early on, and his schedule became part of ours. The moment my husband opened his cage in the morning, it was Fang's job to wake everyone else up. For the next five years, we woke to whiskers on our cheeks, ferret breath in our ears and an eyebrow cleansing. We had just a few minutes to get up; we knew the sneak attack under the sheets to the special spot behind our knees would follow! His morning routine often included taking a shower with whoever would let him in, followed by his devout position at my husband's foot while he tried to get ready for work. He became quite proficient at maneuvering about, with Fang's head plopped steadfast on his foot. When it was time to go, both of them would ready themselves at the top of the stairs in full race position. At my husband's command, "Ready, set, go!" they would race to the bottom, followed by a leaping dance two shared with abandoned joy around the living room. Every single night for years, Fang woke from his nap to come downstairs at exactly 9:10 P.M. and lie at our feet and yawn. He was like a dependable clock with a battery that only slowed with age.

As the months grew into years, Little Fang was never caged. No matter what time of day we arrived home, he was at the door to meet us, with his little neck cocked up, as if to say, "What took you so long?" When insulinoma struck at the age of five, our lives revolved around his medicine, chicken gravy, and special feedings. His needs were always met before our own.

Following his first surgery, a partial pancreatectomy and adrenalectomy, Fang went home with the vet to be monitored that first night while still on IVs. The next morning, however, Fang adamantly refused all attempts of care by the staff. Further testing revealed his blood was not clotting. He no longer fought being probed for blood draws; his little body became totally limp, preparing itself for death. When I rushed to his side to hold him, the staff was amazed as Fang lifted his head to kiss me, and within seconds was trying to eat the same food he had refused minutes earlier from the staff! The next two hours brought us to our knees, as the frantic search for a ferret blood donor seemed hopeless. I cradled his little head in the crook of my neck while I rocked him and told him about The Bridge. His little head was soaked by my tears, as I tried to say goodbye to this sweet little soul so soft against my skin. Having only minutes left to live, an angel wearing ferret fur was rushed into the office! The blood transfusion was successful, and Little Fang came home with us to begin the next stage of his battle to live for the people that needed and loved him.

Five months later, and blood tests every two weeks, Fang went full swing into diabetes which is the opposite of insulinoma. In June, we smuggled him into our vacation destination, four states away. Three days into our vacation, we woke to find Fang in agony and unable to walk. Three visits to three vets in that area led us to throw our belongings into our car and rush back home. We couldn't let him die so far away from home! We needed our own vet, who knew and loved Fang. The two-day drive was excruciating, as we tried to prepare ourselves once more for his death. When we arrived at the vet's office on Sunday night after hours, we were shocked to discover that at that very moment Fang began walking and even running! His blood tests revealed a totally normal count for the first time in almost two years! Blessings like this make us humble, but this one was not to be ours for long. Within three weeks the Insulinoma returned, and he was again taking Prednisone.

In November we decided to have another surgery to buy some more time. We brought a friend's ferret along in case a donor was needed. The vet also had another ferret ready as a backup. We went into this with depleting money reserves, but with the vow that we would do anything necessary for Little Fang. Within minutes our hearts were heavy with the news that a new tumor was encased in his liver. There was no hope; there was nothing the vet could do. We were told that Little Fang would bless our lives for six more weeks at the most.

Fuzzbean Crossing

Preparing for Christmas, we hung Fang's little stocking with ours, and wrapped his special presents. This Christmas, his stocking was filled with treats he hadn't been able to have because of his illness. There was lots of red licorice and the special doggy treats he used to steal. He surprised us all by being with us over the holidays, but soon grew increasingly weak. He could no longer drag my husband's tennis shoe down the hall which he loved to do. We would find it halfway to its destination, and would carry it up for him and gently place it beside him. Fang slept most of the time, and had to be carried up and down the stairs.

In the afternoon of February 15, 2001, we found him lying at the bottom of the stairway. He was lethargic and limp. He refused all food. He had come all the way down to find us to let us know it was his time. Vets say that ferrets will tell you when it is time, and they do. It is then that we have to be strong and do what is best for them. We took turns holding him that night, but as the night grew on, he wanted to be alone with his blankie and in his own bed. We were up every hour, dreading the feel of a cold little body, dreading to know it was still to come. I had arranged for a friend to drive me to a local vet the next morning because my husband had to work that day. He is a working cowboy on a ranch that had a huge cattle drive scheduled. When my friend and I arrived at the vet's office, I was surprised to see my husband's truck there! When his boss found out Fang was going to be put to sleep, the cattle drive was delayed so my husband could be with Fang in his last moments. We took turns holding Little Fang, trying to say goodbye. When I asked, "Who would be Daddy's shadow in the morning?" my husband took out his big red bandana and sobbed. Everybody there was crying, and Little Fang was reminded one last time how much he was loved. He was only 6½ years old.

As we always said around our house, "he was loved beyond words." I wish this kind of love could come into the hearts of humans everywhere; to give all pets a chance to become a participating member of the family; to have the opportunity to shine its' own special light. The rewards are immeasurable. My poems[23] express our love for Little Fang and I know he is pleased. I know it is his hope that others might open their hearts to a little animal with so much love of its' own to give. It is my wish for you, that you might be one of the lucky ones to experience it.

Love,
Liz
Colorado

 Purchase an over-the-door shoe rack or a small two-tier shoe shelf to put on your closet shelf instead of on the floor. This will keep shoes away from your ferrets who love to eat any kind of rubber, including the insoles of shoes.

---

[23] See Liz's poems throughout the book.

LITTLEONE

It's been ten days since I lost my Littleone and I still feel like it happened today. I never knew anything could hurt this much and my heart is broken. Littleone wriggled into my heart the first time I held her and she will stay there always. God, please look for Littleone, my little sable girl, and tell her how much I miss her. I will cherish every moment we had together. Tell her I'll be at The Bridge to get her one day but, until then, I'll hold her in my heart.

> Littleone's Mom,
> Janet
> Rhode Island

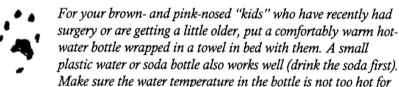

For your brown- and pink-nosed "kids" who have recently had surgery or are getting a little older, put a comfortably warm hot-water bottle wrapped in a towel in bed with them. A small plastic water or soda bottle also works well (drink the soda first).

Make sure the water temperature in the bottle is not too hot for their sensitive skin and the top is screwed on tight. Remove the bottle after one to two hours when it gets cold. If your furkids get sick or have had recent surgery, it is possible for them to go into hypothermic shock very quickly if their body temperature drops a few degrees.

LOVE

Yesterday our shelter rescued several ferrets from a backyard breeder. Today we lost a tiny girl. She was a newborn, about 5 to 6 weeks old, with many problems. We named her Love. We did all we could, but it wasn't enough. She died in my arms this morning without ever having a chance to live.

God, please look for her, she is a tiny panda girl. I know Bullwinkle, Ginger and Mr. Peabody will take care of her. Peabody can teach her how to dance, Bullwinkle can teach her how to hide toys and Ginger can be her new mom. We only knew her for a day, but we loved her enough for a lifetime.

Barb and George
Maryland

 Did you ever notice that your ferret's whiskers are flat against the sides of their face when they are relaxed or sleeping? When ferrets are awake and fully alert, the whiskers stick straight out from their muzzle.

LUCKY

Every time I go to the mall I stop at the pet store to admire and hold the baby ferrets, and then I leave. Today was no different—I looked at the beautiful kits, browsed the store a bit and on my way out I took one more look because they are so precious. I started talking to the sales clerk about my five fuzzies. She asked me if knew anything about sick ferrets and I said I did because I have lived with ferrets for almost seven years. She led me to the back office and there, in an aquarium, was a teeny tiny sable kit, sleeping in a ball. When I picked him up he was so cold and weighed next to nothing. I pinched up his skin to see if he was dehydrated. His little neck skin stayed up as if it were made of wax. I told the clerk and the store manager that this baby was severely dehydrated and if he didn't get immediate treatment he would die. The clerk told me they had given the baby antibiotics in his water but he had not been drinking the water. She said they had not taken him to see a vet. I said I would take him to my vet and they agreed.

I put the little boy under my sweater to keep him warm and to feel secure on the way to the hospital. I called him Lucky, thinking this would be his lucky day because I was determined to get him the help he so desperately needed. As I gave him some water in a syringe he opened his little eyes and looked at me as if to say, "thank you for helping me."

At the hospital he was rushed into a cozy, warm incubator. He was immediately given subcutaneous fluids, intravenous fluids and antibiotics. It was suspected he had ulcers or even ECE. I left him at the hospital, knowing he was in good hands now. Unfortunately, at 8:00 A.M. the next morning, I received a call from the hospital saying that Lucky didn't make it. He was so dehydrated and his tiny little body, weighing only one-half pound, just couldn't take any more. I had even made up a bed for him when he comes home to me.

God, please look out for this little guy. He needs so much love that he never got while he was here on Earth. If my love would have been enough to make him live, he be home with me right now. Please let him know how sorry I am I couldn't save him and that although we were only together a very short while, I loved him very much. Please also tell Lucky that after I stopped crying, I got mad. He will have not died in vain. I have filed a formal complaint against the store. I will do everything in my power to see this doesn't happen again.

> I miss you little Lucky boy,
> Sue
> Georgia

When giving occasional treats of fruits and vegetables to your slinky ones, make sure to chop finely or mash thoroughly so they won't choke on anything. Bananas, strawberries, pears, cantaloupe, watermelon, tomatoes and cucumbers are favorite treats. For a different taste treat, chop green pepper, broccoli or carrots finely and see if your ferrets will eat them. All treats should be given sparingly, once a week or less. Fruits contain sugar and sugar is not good for your ferret's teeth and vegetables are not easily digested by ferrets.

LUCKY

It is with a sad heart that I let you know that Lucky, a hob[24] of 9 to 10 years of age, and one of the first of seventeen we rescued from western Michigan, has departed to the Rainbow Bridge. He left on Friday, May 18, 2001. God, please make sure he finds the rest of the crew who are at The Bridge.

When Lucky first came to us, he was an extreme biter. His previous caretaker was afraid of him and had abused him. At that time, Lucky lived in a cage in an unventilated shed. Through tender loving care for Lucky by my daughter, my son and myself, he became more trusting, but remained very afraid of people. His five years with us was a time of love.

Lucky, I love you and I will see you again at the Rainbow Bridge.

Rev. Ronald
Michigan

Human nail clippers work well for clipping ferret nails. Make sure you have plenty of light while doing the nail clipping and look for the vein running through the center of the nail. Do not clip too close to the vein. Clip nails at an angle, the same angle that the foot touches the floor. Nail clipping is best done with two people, one to hold the ferret and the other to clip the nails. However, one person can learn to do this task. Try putting some Ferretone or cat hairball remedy on your ferret's belly. Lay the ferret on your lap on his/her back and clip the nails while they are busy licking off the treat. Another way is to sit in a comfortable chair with a tube of cat hairball remedy between your knees with the cap off. Put the ferret on your lap and let them lick the hairball remedy while you clip nails. Your knees also work to squeeze a little more hairball remedy from the tube. This works great!

---

[24] Male unaltered ferret.

MAJOR BURNS

Last night around 1930 hours, Major Burns departed this life to command his troops at The Bridge. The healing he so desperately needed could only be found on the other side. He had been sick a long time, suffering from insulinoma surgery and a resulting cataract on his left eye. He'd had one, then another, adrenalectomy and a splenectomy. He seemed much better these past few weeks but a few days ago he became listless and had a distended abdomen. When he became incontinent last night, he looked up at me as if to say, "Daddy, it's time for me to go."

He was in my arms as he slipped away at the vet's office. The vet asked if I wanted to be there as he helped him over The Bridge, and I replied, "No, I don't want to be here at all. However, I'm going to be here! I wanted Major to die with dignity and looking at the face of the man who loved him. I should not cry, he was ready and suffering. But for me, I cry. He was my first ferret and still is.

Major Burns came to me in December 1995 as my first rescue. Discovered in an apartment parking lot, the director of the local animal shelter and personal friend said, "I know you've had experience with ferrets. I have one here that isn't doing too well and thought you might take him for a few days, help him get settled down, until I can get him placed." At the time I was ferretsitting two of my son's ferrets, and my friend thought maybe Major would do better in their company until he was adopted.

Major finally got adopted last night by all his brothers and sisters who've already gone to The Bridge. Major was always the alpha ferret around here and, well, being a major and all, he may just want to take over! God, just find him a white slightly worn tennis shoe and he'll be happy. He has his favorite pajama bottoms already with him, so he'll be fine. I don't know about his Dad, though. I didn't know this would hurt so much. Major Burns, be a good boy now; your daddy will miss you.

Tuck
Texas

MANDRAKE

Back in the early days of our growing ferret family, Jack and I took turns choosing the babies we would have join us. Since I had chosen my silver mitt the year before, Jack had decided we should next add the darkest colored sable we could find. We already had our White Wizard, so it was time to add the Dark Wizard. It took a while to find her, but one day Jack came home and told me he thought he had found her at a local pet store. We both went to look and ended up bringing Mandrake and her sister, Aislyn[25], home. The two of them were so very tiny and were dubbed "the littles" as they toddled around their new home and met their new brothers and sisters, who appeared enormous in comparison.

Mandrake was the only one of our ferrets who actually barked. One day when I walked into her room and startled her, she made a loud noise I had never heard before. She only did this a couple times before she realized that no harm would come to her in her new home. Mandrake never did live up to her name. Although she was dark in color, she was bright and gentle and kind in spirit. She remained a dark sable throughout her life, though her mask would become more pronounced at different times of the year. Her most striking feature was her eyes—they were big, gentle and brown, reminding me of a doe. She never hurt a soul—human or fuzzy— and she lived her life with a tranquil, quiet joy that spread throughout our home and touched us all.

Every ferret has their favorite toys and for Mandy it was tennis balls. She would grab them by the fuzz and busily move them to where they belonged. Apparently, they each had a specific spot that only she knew about and it was her job to make sure they got there. She worked so hard at this. When it came to "raisin time," while the others crowded around climbing over each other trying to get theirs first, Mandy would patiently wait for her turn. She was good about using the litter box 100% of the time, unlike the others. Even when she felt sick following her surgery, she made sure to get to the

---

[25] See Aislyn's story elsewhere in the book.

litter box in her hospital cage. She was truly an angel here on Earth. Mandy would have been 6 years old on January 27, 2000.

Mandy, I hope you know I was trying to make your life better by choosing surgery for you and I thought you would be better in time for Christmas. I know how much you missed Aislyn when she left. I hoped you would wait a while before you joined her, but I guess you knew better. I will be thinking of all of you together again for Christmas, hoping you have a tree to play in with lots of presents.

My darling Mandy, I miss you more than words can say. Your tennis ball is still by the rocking chair, just where you left it. It belongs there, so there it will stay. You will always be in our hearts.

With all my love,
Mom Lucie and Dad Jack
Florida

Don't use fabric softener or scented dryer sheets when washing your ferret's bedding including hammocks, blankets, sleep sacks, etc. Ferrets have a highly developed sense of smell and a delicate respiratory system. Look for laundry detergents without a strong scent or, better yet, no scent at all.

MAXIE

Yesterday I picked up a little ferret from the local pet shop to foster and nurse back to health. She had been turned in to the store by her family and was very sick. Unfortunately, she was too far gone and I could not save her. Her previous caretakers had neglected her and had never even given her a name. We called her Maxie.

God, she doesn't know anyone up there so if you could please help her find someone to help her and show her the ropes. She is a cute little sable who gave me kisses the first time I picked her up, even when she was extremely sick. Though I knew her less than twenty-four hours, she will always be in my memory and I will consider her mine. Tell her she wasn't an unwanted unloved ferret. I have never had a ferret go to the Rainbow Bridge and I am in tears. I will look for her when I get there. Tell her to wait at The Bridge for me and I will meet her again one day.

Tracy
Nevada

To warm up a sick or recuperating ferret, put one cup of uncooked rice in a clean sock and heat it in the microwave for about thirty seconds. Tie a knot in the top of the sock and wrap it in a thin towel and lay it next to your ferret. Warmed rice will stay heated for approximately two hours. Just pop the sock back in the microwave to rewarm it when it cools off. Feel the warm sock to see if it is comfortably warm and not too hot.

MAXIMILIAN

Maximilian, my dear friend and companion, has left this world for the Rainbow Bridge. Max was born February 10, 1995, and died peacefully in his sleep on January 8, 2002. He was afflicted with cardiomyopathy.

Max was always free roaming and never understood what a cage was. Our house was his house and I lived here with his permission. We spent our last day together with Max sleeping in my lap. His exit from this world, thank goodness, was without pain or suffering. I loved Max dearly and no matter what happened in my life, he was always there. He was my comfort and my strength. It is now after 3 A.M. and I have yet to go to sleep, so deep is my loss of such a wonderful friend.

Rest in peace Max, one day I'll meet you at Rainbow Bridge.

C.B.
Arkansas

P.S. To make sure I never have to leave my little fur baby, Max was taken to the cemetery where I own plots. My daughter distracted the sexton and I buried Max next to where I will be one day. I planted a little dwarf spruce to mark his grave and also to keep the sexton from getting suspicious about freshly disturbed earth. Last weekend when I went to the cemetery to spend a few minutes with Max, the sexton came over to me and said he had noticed that my little spruce tree was getting uneven sunlight and was beginning to grow more on one side than the other. He then trimmed and shaped the tree for me. He also told me that he knew the little tree had some very special meaning to me, but he wasn't going to ask any questions. He just smiled and said he would always give the tree special attention.

MEEP

I took Meep to our vet yesterday and he found a large mass in Meep's abdomen. He recommended that I schedule surgery as soon as possible. We force-fed Meep through the weekend and he was responding fairly well. He had a little more energy and wanted his raisin ration. I waited while the doctor did the surgery. Instead of a tumor which could be removed, the doctor found lymphosarcoma which had spread through Meep's intestines. The doctor said there was nothing that could be done to cure Meep and we made the difficult decision to let Meep pass without waking. It is one of the hardest things I've ever had to do.

Meep was our first ferret baby and was so sweet and such a people ferret. He always greeted people when they came to the door. He had definite ideas about where my husband's socks belonged, his special spot where he wanted his raisin and another where he wanted his tasty vitamins.

I brought Meep home with me to bury him on the mountain lot where we will be building our home next summer. Daisy sniffed him for a long while and came back several times as if to be sure he was really gone, then promptly nipped my ankle. God, watch out for my sweet boy; we will miss him so much.

Karla
New York

 For longer shelf life, keep ferret food tightly sealed in the refrigerator or freezer using a plastic freezer bag or plastic container. If you use large twenty-pound bags of food, immediately divide up the food into smaller containers or freezer bags. Exposure to light or air deteriorates pet food quickly.

MISS KITTY

Yesterday morning around 10:00 A.M., my sister's 6-year-old ferret, Miss Kitty, passed gently away in our arms with the help of her wonderful vet. She was a wonderful roommate to my sister during the five and one-half years they shared an apartment. Kitty was a warm, fuzzy busybody to come home to. She accepted the addition of a husband, a dog and a house, but not before establishing who was boss. They were a happy family. Kitty was happiest when she was begging for Cheerios and stealing the shower drain, and loved curling up in her sweatshirt in the corner, dreaming the day away. She was active and up to the usual ferrety things up until just a few days before she died.

She developed insulinoma about seven months ago and was doing well on Prednisone and Brewers Yeast[26]. Kitty also had some suspected heart problems. She stopped eating and drinking a few days ago and had to be handfed and medicated. She continually grew weaker and unable to get around. Kitty perked up some on Easter Sunday after church, giving kisses and being interested in the goings on around her and even ate half of a Cheerio. I think it was her way of saying one last goodbye to us while she could. We knew there was not much hope of a recovery with any quality of life for her and knew she wasn't happy being immobile. So, with heavy hearts, we decided to end her suffering and let her rest peacefully.

She was buried in a fluffy pink towel with a picture of her and my sister tucked between her paws. She was a silver mitt who had turned almost white and she always looked good in pink! As we laid her in her little grave, the chimes of the church in town began to play. It was very fitting for such a solemn occasion. She will be greatly missed and always remembered.

Laura
Oklahoma

---

[26] See the appendix for a description of this supplement.

MISTIE SIOUX

She arrived without a name, not knowing how to play and be a ferret, and not knowing a free life without bars. She would soon come to know all these things.

One day while teaching a computer class at a local college, I began chatting with one of the office staff. I mentioned I had ferrets, and she said she had inherited a ferret from her son when he had left home for school. This little girl ferret lived a solitary and very lonely life in a cage most of the time, unable to exercise, play and explore as ferrets love to do. The woman was getting ready to retire; she wanted to travel and didn't want to be stuck with a ferret. I agreed to take the ferret and give her a good home.

A few days later, after class one day, I brought home a petite and beautiful sable ferret girl. Before we arrived home, I named her Mistie Sioux. She was such a tiny thing, pretty as a princess and all princesses need a proper name.

Over the months Mistie blossomed into such an astonishing ferret, learning to play, explore, cuddle and run with the others. She enjoyed her free roaming life out of a cage forever. She was such a joy to have around.

In 1996 she had insulinoma surgery and was generally healthy until her death in 1998. I was extremely lucky to have lived with such a delicate princess for six years.

> I miss and love you baby,
> Mom
> Virginia

Inspect your home for loose or broken screens in windows and doors. Look for doors that open easily with a good push of a nose. These are easy exits for snoopy ferrets. Check behind appliances and inside and under kitchen and bathroom cabinets for any small openings. Repair or secure all openings.

MOCHA

It came too soon; he wasn't even 4 years old yet. Mocha had been ill since February, seen three vets, and was taking all kinds of medications. Apparently, it was his time. I prayed a few months ago for him to hold on a bit longer, maybe another year or two, but it was not to be. Tuesday I had to help him to The Bridge. I have never been through a more agonizing event in my life. It was so quick; one second he was licking his favorite vitamins, the next he was at The Bridge. The tears have not stopped yet and probably won't for a long while.

He was my alpha ferret and Mocha is the reason I love ferrets so much. He was the teacher of terrible tricks, the raisin runner, the educator of everything I didn't want the other ferrets to know, the flinger of Flagyl[27] (he was very good at that). I am trying to remember the good and not the bad. I remember someone saying, "Don't cry because it's over, but smile because it happened."

God, please show him all the great spots for munchies and fun and where the plastic bags can be found. Bags were his favorite toy. He'd jump on the bag as if it attacked him and then run inside and beat the tar out of it from the inside. The bags didn't last long, so I hope there's a good supply up there. He was a very friendly ferret and I think he'll make friends quickly.

But God, most of all, please tell him how much I will always love him and miss him, and that his roommates miss him, too. Please, tell him I did everything I could to save him.

Angela
Connecticut

---

[27] See the appendix for a description of this medication.

MONKEY

Monkey didn't stand out in a crowd. He didn't do tricks like some of the others such as rolling over, standing up tall on his back feet, fetching and hiding his favorite toys or kissing your face until it tickled like crazy. He didn't lie at your feet until you picked him up and smothered him with kisses and hugs. He wasn't the first one up in the morning or evening to greet me when I arrived home from work. He didn't run really fast and do a flying tackle to attach himself to your leg. What, then, made him so special?

I was introduced to Monkey, my "Monkey Boy" as I later affectionately called him, in May 1995. The name Monkey fit him. With his long legs and body, he looked just like a real monkey. He lived in a small trailer that was the office of a local nursery in the middle of a shopping center parking lot. The trailer was not air conditioned, even though we were in the midst of a typical East Coast heat wave of 90° weather. When I saw the conditions in the trailer, I was very concerned about Monkey's safety. He was in very small cage where he could not move around freely or stand upright. There were wood chips on the cage floor and no place for a litter box. There was no soft bedding for him to curl up in to sleep. Scattered around the trailer were several containers of chemicals along with car batteries and other dangerous materials—too easily accessible to a curious ferret. Sometimes Monkey was let out of the cage to roam freely around the trailer, with an open door to the shopping center parking lot and all the hazards there. His environment consisted of way too many hazardous conditions to count. Monkey was even left in the trailer alone each night when the nursery closed. I was so concerned for Monkey's welfare that I went back to the nursery a few days later under the pretense of wanting to purchase some shrubs for the garden. I really just wanted to see if Monkey was doing all right. I went home feeling helpless and concerned. What could I do to help him?

The day the temperature soared to 96°, I thought about Monkey all day while I was at work. I drove directly to the nursery after work to check on Monkey and asked the young man who kept him if he would be willing to let me take Monkey home on a temporary basis, just to get him through the hot weather. I was afraid he would not have survived much longer in the kind of temperatures we were currently experiencing. Luckily, he agreed to let me take him. I was unprepared to take Monkey home and had no carrier with me, but was determined to take him away from all this before the young man changed his mind. I rushed to the car and looked inside to see what I could fashion to hold him securely until I made the ten to fifteen minute ride home. My soft sided briefcase was the only thing available. I quickly dumped the contents onto the floor and put Monkey inside, zipping it securely. I then placed the briefcase on the floor of the back seat, knowing this was the safest place for him during the ride home.

In his new temporary quarters, Monkey quickly became acclimated to his new surroundings and the several other furry kids who lived here. The young man visited Monkey twice briefly during the next few weeks but then came no more. I was very relieved as time passed because I had become very attached to Monkey's sweet and happy personality. He was playful, but not aggressive, and immediately fit right in with the others. He was content to have others like himself to socialize and sleep with.

In April 1997, it was discovered that Monkey had cancer, some of which was inoperable. I did not know at the time how much longer it would take for the cancer to grow and have more of an effect on him. He was active and healthy for a time, but several weeks later I began to notice visible tumors, first on his neck and then underneath his front leg. He had already lost most of his hair and began losing weight. He became so gaunt that his ribs were quite prominent through his thinning skin. Although I watched him worsen day by day, he still had extremely bright eyes and such an invincible spirit. He never complained. It was as if no matter how frail his body became, it would continue to serve him forever.

Each morning and evening, Monkey would come downstairs all sleepy eyed and sit on his special rug in the kitchen in front of the microwave oven. There he would wait patiently while I heated his food. For several weeks, I mixed different kinds of baby food and herbal supplements together in an effort to lower his protein intake. I hoped this would relieve some of the strain on his weakening kidneys. His body was unable to properly process the food he ate and he became a walking skeleton. I watched him lose weight week by week until I thought his spindly legs would no longer support his body weight. Miraculously, they continued to do so right to the end. He slept most of the time during the last few weeks but was so alive when he was awake. He tried to play a little each day but would tire quickly. I carried him up and down the stairs so he would not get too exhausted. I laid him gently within the folds of the soft comforter that was his bed to make his fragile body as comfortable as possible.

At approximately 9:30 A.M. on Monday, August 18, 1997, 4-year-old Monkey peacefully crossed the Rainbow Bridge at home in his sleep. He will now be able to romp again with the others who went before him.

Today the rug in front of the microwave stands empty. I look frequently for that beautiful trusting face waiting for me to take the hunger away, waiting for me to make everything better. I tried my best, Monkey, to make you comfortable, to help you heal, but God had other plans for you. Your face is only in my memory and in my heart now, where I will fondly remember how special you really were. You are finally at rest now, my very special Monkey Boy.

Mommy
Virginia

 Not all hair loss on your ferret is related to adrenal disease (for more information on this disease, see the appendix). Ferrets go through seasonal changes and you will notice the hair falls out periodically and regrows back within a short time.

MR. EDWARD

After a valiant two-year battle with cancer, Mr. Edward went to the Rainbow Bridge in his sleep at noon today.

One Saturday afternoon in 1997, our son Kevin was working at a mall pet store. A woman came in carrying a small carrier which she put down and then promptly left the store. When Kevin opened the carrier, he found a very thin chocolate ferret who could barely walk due to cage paralysis. Kevin brought home this pathetic looking creature and we named him Mr. Edward.

Mr. Edward was a lap ferret who gave lots of kisses and loved ferret pouches. He looked like ET but he had the heart of a lion. At first he was a social ferret but we had to put him by himself for the last year. He had freedom to roam the house in the evening and staked out his own place in the kitchen. He managed to remove and hide all the potatoes to clear his own spot. We added a pouch for him to sleep in. When he wanted to be picked up, he would sit at your feet and look up at you until you picked him up. He loved to crawl into our bed and sleep at night.

He is now romping with his strange gait at the Rainbow Bridge. Goodbye good friend, you taught us so much.

RIP Mr. Edward - 5/7/00
Harry and Zora Mae
Georgia

Two blue dots behind your ferret's right ear mean they were born at Marshall Pet Products, Inc., ferret breeding facility located in New York State. Marshall ferrets are altered and descented before they are shipped to pet stores.

Mischievous One in Planter Pot

WHISPERS

In the dark,
when all was quiet;
a gentle whisper
in the night.

I thought I heard it;
was it true?
"I'm okay, Mommy,"
... was it you?

My ferret angel
must have come,
to take a break
from having fun.

To tell his Mommy
he's all right;
this little whisper
in the night.

- Liz Blackburn

MR. NOBLE MAN

Dear God,
   Please welcome my beloved Noble to your realm. He left this evening quite unexpectedly. I was at work and when I came home, he had already arrived at The Bridge. My only comfort at the moment is that Noble was healthy and happy for the last of his time with me. He greeted each new day with curiosity and eagerness to explore all of its nooks and crannies.
   God, please tell Noble that I love him very much. The others remaining are going to be lost without him. Please show him where the food is. It doesn't matter what kind, Mr. Noble just loved food. Noble also loved silky-soft sleepy sacks that were too small for him. It was quite funny watching him get himself into his favorite sack. Please help him find his friends who are already there.

Karen
North Carolina

Make sure to keep ferrets away from toxic substances such as cleaners and bleach. When cleaning, keep the ferrets in their room or cage until floors are dry and toxic cleaners are put safely inside a locked cabinet. You may want to look for an electric hard surface cleaner called the Eureka Enviro Steamer that uses plain water to produce steam. This disinfects the kitchen, bathroom, ferret room and any other rooms without carpeting. It does a great job—it's fast and easy to use and you don't have to worry about toxic cleaners. Look for the steam cleaner at department stores, small appliance stores or home improvement centers.

MR. PEABODY

It is with an extremely heavy heart that we said goodbye to Mr. Peabody today. He had a stroke not long ago and, this morning, he just gave up. We took him to the vet and he was helped on his journey.

Mr. Peabody was a wonderful big albino boy. He wasn't much for toys but, boy, could he dance! I've never seen such a happy animal—he dooked and danced circles around the rest. His favorite thing was to try to drag and stash all humans under the sofa. He was such a joy and we were so blessed to know him. We will miss his silliness, but it has been a while since he danced. We know he's probably giving dancing lessons at the Rainbow Bridge.

God, please have Mr. Peabody look for his friends who are already there. Mr. Peabody has his favorite sleep sack with him, but he's willing to share.

We're all brokenhearted, it's so very hard to say goodbye. Mr. Peabody, you'll always be in our hearts. We miss you terribly.

Barb, George, and Joe
Maryland

Avoid using any kind of wood chips or other small animal bedding for ferrets. These are dangerous to your ferret's respiratory system and can cause chronic respiratory disease, asthma and possibly oral cancers. Use small blankets, old T-shirts, or sweats instead. These are nice and soft and your ferret will enjoy curling up and sleeping in them.

MURRAY

Tonight there will be a new star in the sky as Murray makes his way to the Rainbow Bridge. He came to us as a foster but he was part of our family. He wasn't a big guy but he was a strong old man. He didn't take anything from anybody and loved to dook and dance.

God, please help Murray find his friends who went to The Bridge before him so they can welcome him. They will want the news from home. Tell them all we love them and miss them; we will meet again someday.

Goodnight sweet Murray,
Lydia and Ben
Michigan

Keep holiday ornaments and decorations out of reach of curious noses and mouths, especially things like fake holly berry decorations. One Christmas, one of the ferrets ate several fake red "berries" and pooped red berries for hours. Luckily, the berries disagreed with him and were eliminated quickly. Otherwise, we may have had to make an emergency trip to the vet to get them surgically removed. As soon as I found out the berries were consumed, I gave him some cat hairball medicine to help the elimination. All the greenery was quickly thrown away. Keep real plants, like poinsettias and mistletoe, out of reach on a table or on the mantel. See the appendix for other common toxic household plants.

NIPPER

My little Nipper couldn't bear the loss of her Sammy[28] and joined him at the Rainbow Bridge exactly a week after he crossed on November 24, 2001. My house is empty now and so is my heart. I probably will get more ferrets one day, but right now it's just too hard. I miss all of them so much.

Diane
Florida

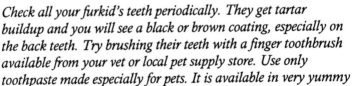

Check all your furkid's teeth periodically. They get tartar buildup and you will see a black or brown coating, especially on the back teeth. Try brushing their teeth with a finger toothbrush available from your vet or local pet supply store. Use only toothpaste made especially for pets. It is available in very yummy malt, poultry or beef flavor. Tooth scalers should be used with caution so as not to scrape away the tooth enamel and are better left to your vet. During your next vet visit, ask them to look at the tartar buildup on your ferret's teeth and recommend when tooth cleaning should be done.

---

[28] See Sammy's story elsewhere in the book.

ODIE

Last week I made the difficult decision I knew one day I would have to make. Odie, the one who made me fall in love with ferrets, was helped across The Bridge. Odie was over 10 years old. She was diagnosed with insulinoma two years ago and had been taking Prednisone and Proglycem[29]. She did extremely well until about two months ago when she began to go downhill. The week before last she really started to slide and I knew it was time. She is now happily playing with her brothers and sisters at The Bridge.

Odie and her sister traveled everywhere with me. She had seen the Statue of Liberty, went skiing with me in Colorado where she tunneled in the snow, drove from Texas to Miami, and lived through several hurricanes in St. Croix. She was the smallest adult ferret I have ever seen; she weighed slightly over one pound at her heaviest.

Odie was the alpha ferret and she would often drag the much larger boys around. She was also the smartest. I could tell her to pick up her toys and she would start moving them around. What I found so amazing is how she got everyone else to help as well. Of course, she only relocated the toys, occasionally taking them back to the ferret room. She also knew her name as well as all the other ferrets' names. I could ask her where Little Bear was, and she would take me to her. Odie's favorite toy was a black and white spotted ball. We went through dozens of balls in the ten years she was with us.

As time passed and I slowly lost my fur babies to cancer and disease, I began to believe that Odie would outlive all of them; she was determined to remain the alpha ferret. She will always be the alpha ferret of my heart.

Amy
St. Croix
U.S. Virgin Islands

---

[29] See the appendix for a description of this medication.

OLDGUY

It is entirely too soon to be doing this again. We had to take OldGuy in and have him helped across The Bridge this morning—April 12, 2000—at 11:00 A.M. He was about 6 years old.

We got him from a ferret shelter on December 30, 1999. He was not considered adoptable because he had so little time left and a botched adrenal surgery before coming in. We knew we only had a little time with him, but we loved him so much.

He started losing weight a few weeks ago and I started supplementing his food with canned food. It worked for a couple weeks, until he quit eating on his own a few days ago. I tried syringe feeding and last night he refused even that.

I was still unsure if it was time; I didn't want it to be. A friend sent me an address to a website about letting go. There, in black and white, were all the signals. OldGuy was telling me, "It's time." My friend told me to let OldGuy know it was all right to go and to give him her love. The next morning, I took him in to the vet. He is at peace now.

So, LittleWhiteGirl, please welcome OldGuy and, for heaven's sake, be nicer to him now than you were here!

We love you, OldGuy,
Goodbye.
Kat
Ohio

 Occasionally, the only way to get a sick or aging ferret to eat is to let them lick canned or baby food from your finger.

Fuzzbean Crossing

OPIE

Dear God,
    As you know, we lost our beloved Opie on Sunday, February 10, 2002. He went in for adrenal tumor surgery, and unfortunately did not recover. I feel so guilty because I wasn't there to hold him in his final moments. Please tell him that we love him and miss him so much. We didn't expect him to join his sister so soon. It's only been two months since we lost her. Tell Opie that his kitty is looking for him.
    I know Opie and his sister have been looking over my shoulder recently because I have felt their presence. Give them hugs and kisses for me and point them in the direction of the Froot Loops—it was always their favorite treat.

Love always,
Holly
Michigan

 Make a simple checklist with your furry carpet surfers' names on it to track ear cleaning and pedicures. This way you can quickly tell which kids have already been done and those who have not. Pick the same day every week that is convenient for you to do this maintenance, such as Saturday or Sunday. Try cleaning ears one week and clipping nails the next. This way, you begin a routine and every week one or the other gets done. Keep the chart handy on the refrigerator so it is easy to locate when you're ready to do the maintenance. The directions for making your own checklist can be found in the Helpful Charts section of the appendix.

PB

He came here from the streets of Bellfontaine, Ohio, abandoned, emaciated and dehydrated. He had eighteen ticks on his body, mostly behind his ears and on his neck. His eyes and nose crusted over with the raging upper respiratory infection that we thought was slowly getting better. I put him in a large carrier in my bedroom near the window so he could get natural light once his eyes were improving. I gave him amoxicillin and soothed his eyes with antibiotic ointment. After one week, his breathing no longer rattled like a battered truck. He had been eating, drinking and eliminating normally. He began demanding attention, usually at 3 A.M., so it was time to move him from my bedside to the kitchen where the whole family could talk to him. I didn't allow anyone else in our house to hold him, afraid that I could not contain the infection. I cuddled him, wrapping him in my favorite old T-shirts and slipped him into pillowcases to keep him warm. He smelled like soggy Fritos even though he had been bathed a few times. I rocked him and crooned to him, bathing his stomach and thighs in warm water to relieve the urine burns on his skin.

"Poor Boy" was all I could say when he first came here but "PB" was his nickname. He had a momma waiting for him, hoping he would recover and go home with her forever. She was going to visit him on Sunday, knowing it would be a few more weeks before he would be well enough to go home. I didn't think he was making much progress and was going to take him to the vet. As I joyfully reached in to give him the stronger antibiotic I was sure would make him better, I found a cold, slightly stiffening body in the soft sleepsack. I jerked my hand back, stunned. Once the shock wore off, I began to grieve.

I was going to have PB cremated but decided instead to bury him next to our kitten who loved the ferrets. I wanted them to have each other for company. I cuddled him close before putting his physical self to rest. I buried PB under the flowerbed in our front yard, carefully removing the top layer of soil and newly growing wildflowers so I could lay them over him. I wrapped him in my son's Winnie the Pooh baby blanket that I had saved for ten years, and put him in a plastic bag to keep the sickness and smell from attracting wild critters.

I cannot believe he has passed on. I'd be only too happy to hear him rattle the door to his cage for attention, no matter what time of day. I am so sorry I wasn't able to cure him, that it just wasn't enough to save his life. He is missed very much. PB was here for only eighteen days and had the best we could give him. I wish I could have seen him get fat and healthy with clear eyes and a nose that didn't have infection clogging it all the time.

Goodbye my Poor little Boy. Forgive those who failed you here on Earth.

Kim
Ohio

 Do your fuzzykins like to play catch and fetch with a bouncing ball? Do they love to grab the ball and drag it backwards to their favorite hiding place? Tennis balls are good for supervised play and bounce well. Always keep the balls out of the ferret's reach, such as in a drawer, when you are not playing with them.
Tennis balls have a fuzzy covering and, since ferrets love to chew on rubber objects, the fuzz could be easily ingested and cause an intestinal blockage. This tip applies to other rubber balls too. Put balls and other rubber toys away so they don't get eaten the minute you are not looking.

PALADIN

Dear God,

Please greet Paladin who died in my arms Christmas Day 2000 from complications of insulinoma. He was over 10 years old.

Paladin was our first old-timer and was 7 years old when he came to live with us. He taught us how wonderful the oldtimers are. Since then, we've opened our hearts to several more oldtimers whose families didn't want them anymore. When we first met Paladin, he was in the ferret playpen with the other ferrets up for adoption at the shelter. He was always passed over because he was too old, even though he danced his best waltz, just a slower version of the weasel war dance.

Paladin was ever so gentle with the younger ferrets and had his favorite two ladies who miss him. He warmly welcomed all newcomers. He taught us the Tickle the Tummy Game and loved to roll in the grass in the warm weather. I miss my TV and computer buddy. I miss the kisses and how he scratched my feet to be picked up and cuddled or to have his tummy tickled.

God, I told Paladin to look for his friends who are already there. He, like all before him, is sorely missed. Our only regret is that we didn't know him when he was younger; he was a treasure.

Barb and George
Maryland

Keep plastic tubes of hand lotion, soap, toothpaste and make-up out of your ferret's reach. Although none of these would taste good to us, ferrets love to eat these things. These items probably wouldn't be toxic but they could give your ferret a large case of indigestion and could induce vomiting.

PATO

I came home from work today to find my sweet baby, Pato, had passed away in his little hammock while I was at work. When I left for work this morning, I kissed him goodbye, told him I loved him and I would be back soon.

When I came home at noon, I went to see the "babies." Pato was lying tucked in his hammock with little chin and paws poking out. He must have crossed The Bridge right after I left because he was no longer warm. God, I don't even want to think about it. My poor precious boy was only 5 years old.

I wrapped Pato in the hammock he loved so well. His daddy and uncle made him a grave in our backyard. His uncle also made him a little cross and his aunt cut roses from the bushes for his grave—all the things I couldn't do because I was crying so hard. Why did he have to leave, especially when I wasn't home? I was only gone four hours. He was fine when I left, just fine.

Pato was my first ferret and the one who taught me to love ferrets so much. He would watch cartoons in bed with his daddy. He would play chase and was very pampered and spoiled. Tonight was supposed to be his tubby night. He loved his baths very much. I told him when I left this morning that everyone would get their manicures and baths when I got home.

Oh dear God, I want my baby back. St. Francis, please hold Pato in your arms so he isn't scared. Tell him his mommy loves him and is sorry she wasn't there when it was his time to leave. I should have been there to hold him. There are so many tears in our household this evening.

Catherine
Utah

PEANUT

God, after a short but vicious battle, Peanut was helped to come see you on Monday, October 8, 2001. Look for her; she will be the very pretty soft-coated girl with no tail. Not that the tail part made her less of a ferret. Please tell her she is missed very much and still loved a lot. Find her a nice soft job that will allow her plenty of free playtime; during her short life, she did not get enough.

Peanut was only 1½ years old and had been in at least three homes and two shelters. When she came here, it was decided that she would stay with us in our shelter forever and get all the love we could find for her. However, that must have not been enough because she left us after only a few short weeks. In those few weeks, I came to love her very much because she was the sweetest girl. She gave the best and wettest kisses any ferret has ever bestowed upon me. So, please give her a warm welcome and tell her that when my time comes, she better be waiting there for me.

JD
Florida

The ferret nose is a wonderful tool. Not only is it good for sniffing out the best treats or sniffing another ferret's rear end, it is also amazingly adept at opening any door whether it's a bathroom, a closet or cupboard door. Make sure to keep doors closed if there are things on the other side that a ferret should not explore. For kitchen and bathroom cupboards, install magnetic locks to keep ferrets out of these dangerous places. Look for Magnetic Tot Loks at hardware and home improvement centers. Childproof locks are not ferret-proof.

PEEDEE

PeeDee was our brave fighter who crossed the Rainbow Bridge Saturday morning.

He was a stray who was picked up in the wilds of Virginia. When I got him, he had a large abscessed tumor and surgery was performed to remove it. The results of the biopsy were devastating—an aggressive malignant cancer. He was given a poor outlook and his life was measured in months. We were aggressive in treating the cancer and PeeDee had two more surgeries. PeeDee got his name because of the location where the tumor began—the prepuce. He lived more than a year after his last surgery.

PeeDee was a handsome fellow. Some people might have called him a typical sable ferret, but I saw in his eyes the will to live, and that he did. He loved the other ferrets and never fought with them. We tried to find a new home for PeeDee, but it just never happened. He developed insulinoma early this year and we began treating him.

About two weeks ago, PeeDee was feeling down. Although he was eating and drinking normally, his energy level was low. We heard a rattle in his chest, sounding like an infection. The vet gave him antibiotics. We were back at the vet's five days later when we noticed enlarged lymph nodes on his back legs. The cancer had returned and attacked his lymph nodes; his lungs and heart were being affected. We monitored him closely through the week and saw some improvement, but on Saturday morning, he crashed. He had no energy and was having difficulty breathing. I couldn't let him suffer and we freed him from his cancer at 7:05 A.M. on October 27, 2001.

It is so difficult every time a shelter ferret dies. I feel like I have failed them because I did not find them a new home. PeeDee was such a good boy and deserved a good home. He is a bright star now and out of pain. I'm going to miss you, big guy.

                                      Lisa
                                      Virginia

PEPE

My PePe went to the Rainbow Bridge today. God, please tell him his buddy will be there looking for him.

PePe was a throw away and we took him into our home to be part of our family. He was the cutest and most loveable little guy you'd ever want to meet. We named him PePe like the cartoon character, PePe le Pew, the lover. That is what my PePe was like—a lover all the way. He always had kisses for anyone who wanted them and, for those who didn't, they got them anyway. PePe was about 6 to 7 years old, we are not sure. He is so missed right now and I am crying so hard.

Please God, watch for my baby PePe and let his friend know he is on his way.

Candy
Illinois

Hide anything with rubber buttons on it such as the TV remote control, the telephone or a lens covering on your camera in a closed cabinet or up on a high shelf out of reach. These are just a few common household items that could be hazardous to your fuzzbuns. They love to eat rubber and will eat a button very quickly and get a blockage, which will probably have to be removed surgically. A foreign object obstruction is very serious and can kill your ferret within a short time. Your ferrets trust you, their caretaker and provider, to keep them safe at all times. This is a mighty big job because each day ferrets discover new and exciting things to get into. It is your job to outsmart the ferrets and it's their nature to outsmart you.

PJATTEN

Dear God,

My gorgeous ferret boy, Pjatten, left me last Friday and I want you to look out for him.

He was approximately 10 years old, maybe older. I rescued him from under a barn in February 1992 and when he was altered, the vet said he thought Pjatten was about 2 years old or possibly older. Pjatten became rather tired in the last six months but there was nothing else wrong with him. He would hardly play with his mate and told the dog not to bother him. He was eating and drinking and occasionally exploring the apartment, although mostly resting. We decided to let him be until he showed signs of illness or became uncomfortable.

However, Pjatten himself made the decision to leave and passed away suddenly, just as he was leaving his basket to take a walk. We gave him a temporary rest under the trees in a beautiful spot of the woods until he can get to you.

Help him find his friends who will be waiting there for him. Take good care of Pjatten, God.

                                      Mom
                                      Sweden

 A group of ferrets is called a "business." Who thought this up anyway? No doubt it was a ferret breeder.

POGO

Pogo, my five and one-half-year-old ferret, had insulinoma and adrenal surgery. Since his energy was still good and he was in fairly good health, I wanted to catch things early. Pogo always hated to go to the vet and was very scared when he had to visit. I knew, however, this was his only chance to survive much longer.

The surgery was Tuesday and it went great. Pogo came out of the anesthesia and even took a few steps that evening. Since he was doing so well, the doctor went home and left him in the hospital alone for the night.

When the doctor arrived at the office the next morning, he noticed that Pogo had recently died and his body was still warm. He had no idea why this happened, but suspected a possible underlying cardiomyopathy.

I feel bad that Pogo died alone in a vet's office, the place he disliked the most. I only hope he died in his sleep. I was prepared for the worst, knowing it was a risky operation, but was still totally blindsided by it.

Pogo leaves his friend behind who looked all over the house for him. I hope and trust Pogo's spirit rejoins his best buddy who died two years ago.

This also closes an era for me. For a long time, a cat and two ferrets were the best buddies I had. I am married now and there are other cats in the household. The ferrets were "illegal aliens" before ferrets were legal in Massachusetts. Now all three are gone and this house feels very empty.

Pogo will be buried in our backyard in Friday, in the same grave where his buddy was buried almost two years ago.

Mason
Massachusetts

POPCORN

Popcorn left for The Bridge yesterday. She was 8½ years old. I rescued Popcorn when she was just a few months old, borrowing my sister's car to drive into Center City Philadelphia, even though I didn't know my way around. I was told to, "come right now or we'll have to get rid of her." That was around Thanksgiving in 1991. I didn't like her name when we first got her, but wasn't going to bother changing it since she was just passing through as a rescue. Well, she ferreted her way into our hearts and was officially adopted on Christmas Day, 1991. By that time I had come to love her name, as it fit her perfectly—Popcorn, my little white bouncy bit of fluff.

A stunning white albino, her fur was almost pure white her entire life and very thick, not thinning and taking on the normal yellow hue of albinos until later in life.

All was ideal until her two dear friends passed away just a few days from each other in the fall of 1995. She became very lonely, so we adopted another ferret to be her friend. She didn't particularly like him very much, but they did grow to become friends. He passed away last summer. She didn't seem particularly lonely this time, so we decided not to put her through getting used to another ferret.

Popcorn had been on borrowed time for a year and a half. We almost put her down around Thanksgiving two years ago due to extreme psychotic behaviors related to adrenal disease. Then she started taking Lupron, which gave her a year and a half of great quality life that she wouldn't have had otherwise.

This past week Popcorn slowly stopped eating. I don't know if she was sick or just decided it was her time to go. She seemed slightly nauseated, but in no particular pain. She slowly lost strength until we gave her the final gift of letting her go yesterday. She left very peacefully, with George and me right by her side. Her body rests beneath a beautiful flowering cherry tree, currently in full bloom, alongside her two best friends. She's wrapped in her favorite fleece shirt, and has a pair of my good socks that she liked to steal.

Hopefully, she has found her friends at The Bridge and is waiting for the day when we can all be together again.

Sadly, Popcorn was my last ferret. There is no more jingle of ferret bells running around the house any longer. Godspeed, my dearest Popcorn.

Nancy
Delaware

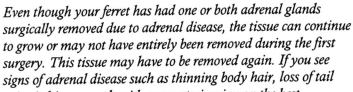

Even though your ferret has had one or both adrenal glands surgically removed due to adrenal disease, the tissue can continue to grow or may not have entirely been removed during the first surgery. This tissue may have to be removed again. If you see signs of adrenal disease such as thinning body hair, loss of tail hair or excessive itching, consult with your veterinarian on the best treatment for your ferret.

PUGSLEY

One of my first adopted ferrets, Pugsley, who came to me huge as a house, recently lost a lot of weight. One day I noticed his little paws were shaking and he was having difficulty breathing. This once roaring, bullying bad boy was now small and frail; as I cuddled him in my arms, he just lay there not moving. I knew in my heart he wanted to go. I considered euthanization, asked questions of the doctor and cried a lot. The decision to euthanize any pet is difficult, painful and heartbreaking. The more I looked at him, the more I realized that tests and doctors weren't the answer for my Puggie. The answer was within me and my ability to say goodbye—my ability to tell him that it was okay to go and to help him on his way. He must have been so scared; I can't imagine how he must have felt. I held him and told him I loved him, that it was okay and that he would be better soon. I said how sorry I was that he couldn't stay longer. I held him, kissed his little head, stroked his little paws and made sure he knew how much I loved him until he drifted off to sleep forever.

I love that little guy and will miss him terribly. I believe I did the right thing and I think my Puggie is going to be better now, better at The Bridge than here in this world with his illnesses.

I'm glad Pugsley was here with me and I'm glad I was there for him. I will see him again someday when I meet my babies at The Bridge.

God, could you please watch for my Puggie. He was a bit of a bully and I know my Chip, who's already there, will remember him. I hope they can get along better at The Bridge than they did here. Puggie likes chicken and rice baby food and heavy cream Thank you, God, for looking out for them both since I can't do it anymore.

Betty
Pennsylvania

QUASIMOTO

Dear Quazi,
  You were giving me the eye in that pet store in West Virginia seven short years ago. All spring and summer, when I went to the pet store, I held you and wished I could take you home. Finally, in the fall when I came in to get you, you were gone.
  On a cold February day, I made a visit to the pet store again and, to my surprise, you were back. Someone couldn't handle you and I quickly took you home this time.
  You were there with me every day. You loved to knock the phone book off the bottom shelf because you knew it didn't belong there. You were there when I was laid off, losing everything. You were there when I lived in that dank basement, making me laugh and licking my nose all the while. You didn't care where we lived, as long as we were together. You came with me to Delaware and lived in the closet because ferrets were not allowed in the building. You moved with me to Maryland and had the run of the bedroom while I renovated the house. You would give me dirty looks and carry the treats I dropped in your hammock to the food bowl. It was as if you were telling me, "Food does not belong in the bed, but in the food bowl." You snorkeled in the snow, raced through your tubes, danced a thousand dances and brought joy to my life. You welcomed a new little brother when Angel brought him home.
  You kept Angel up all night during a blizzard when I was on the road and you first developed insulinoma. You scared her to death. You were the little trooper that took those nasty medications twice each day. You slowly got worse as the medicine lost its effectiveness. You welcomed our next ferret into the household and taught him the ropes, even though you were ill. You slowly grew weaker. You learned to block the medicine with your tongue and would sling it back at us. You gave fewer kisses, slept more and we never knew when we would find you sleeping or seizing. It broke our hearts every day as we watched you get weaker. Finally, you lost the sparkle in your eye and we knew you had had enough.

You kissed me that last morning, snuggled contently on my lap on that short drive to the vet's office. You were a trooper and slowly fell asleep in my arms, your last sleep. You looked so peaceful, lying in the little crib—free at last. You were now at The Bridge, running and playing. You were so soft as we kissed you one last time, covered you up and left.

You can't be gone. You are my son, my little boy, my Quaz monster. We will love you forever and our hearts are breaking every moment of every day. We wish you were here with us again.

Ken and Angel
North Carolina

If you have to give liquid medication, dispense the correct amount into a spoon and have the ferret lick it off. If your ferret doesn't like the taste, put the medication in a spoon with a small amount of canned Hill's a/d Prescription Diet food (available from your vet) or Ferretone (available from pet stores). As a last resort, give the medication in a small plastic syringe (available from your vet) and hold the ferret securely. Slowly and carefully put a few drops into the side of the mouth, between the upper and lower jaw. Do not give the entire amount at once or squirt it directly into the center of the mouth on the tongue. This could cause choking or inhaling of the fluid into the lungs. If giving a small amount of liquid medication such as .1cc, also try dipping the end of the syringe in some Hill's a/d first and then administer to your ferret. This works like a charm.

RASCAL

I had to help one of my babies on her journey to the Rainbow Bridge today. Rascal was a rescue who was found left behind in a mobile home when the family just moved out. Her age was unknown, but my vet figured she was an older lady. She was the most gentle of spirits and she came into my life just after I had lost a ferret to insulinoma a month earlier. I also thought Rascal was the other ferret reincarnated. She shared so much of the same temperament, even down to loving toes fresh from the shower. The only difference between the two was the coloring. One was a beautiful sable; the other, a perfect albino.

Just over a year ago, Rascal developed insulinoma. For a while, I was able to maintain her on the minimum dosage of Prednisone. About six months ago, I had to increase the dosage. In the last week, her blood sugar was extremely low. Saturday morning, I woke up with a feeling that it was "Rascal's day." I was unable to get her to take her medicine and then the seizures started. I rushed her to the vet but we were unable to stabilize her. I had made a promise to Rascal that when the time came, I would make it easy on her and I kept that promise. Rascal passed easily over The Bridge where I know she is pain free and whole again. She is now resting peacefully beside a beautiful camellia that is in full bloom. In the summer, she will have a gardenia on the other side of her.

Barbara
Alabama

 Take a few minutes out of your busy schedule right now to hug and play with your ferrets. You'll be happy you did.

REBECCA "BECCA" SIOUX

Over in the corner by the window sat four little furry bodies nestled close together in a basket. They fit so perfectly together and were enjoying each other's company so much, it was hard to tell that the two boys and two girls had been given up by their families a few days before and were currently living at the shelter. I'm sure they were now trying to figure out where they were and where all those new smells were coming from. Since only their little faces were looking up at me, they looked like baby birds in a nest, although none of them were actually babies at the time. Rebecca was a dark sable and absolutely gorgeous.

I wasn't planning to adopt another ferret at that time back in May 1994 because I had four others already at the time and had my hands full. I certainly could not consider taking four more home at once, which would double my ferret population. I was also trying to move within a couple of weeks and was definitely too busy to devote the extra time necessary to socialize four new ferrets with the ones already at home. I couldn't take my eyes off these four beautiful furry kids and didn't hesitate much longer, knowing that I had to give them a permanent home. I just figured that four more would be twice as much fun.

From the beginning, Becca was such a joy and a great addition to our fuzzy family. It was such a delight watching her enjoy her new life. She loved playing with all the other ferrets and settled into her new life with ease. I always though she would have been a great mother if she had ever had kits because she loved to groom all the others, including me. She would clean your ears, your eyes and your whole face until you sparkled.

Late in the fall of 1998, Becca stopped eating and drinking on her own and was diagnosed with cancer. I had to hand feed her warmed food every few hours so she would get the nutrients necessary to sustain her. I moved her into my bedroom and out of the ferret room so the others would not pick on her. Becca was now approximately 8 years old and had lived a happy life with me and the other sixteen furrballs for almost five years. Just before

Christmas, I could see that Becca's cancer was progressing rapidly and was heartbroken to know there was no chance of recovery. This was a very difficult time because I had lost one of the other "baby birds," a few days before Christmas last year.

God got an extra special gift this past Christmas—a new angel. Rebecca Sioux crossed the Rainbow Bridge to become one of God's furry angels on December 24, 1998.[30] I know her three friends were waiting for her in that little basket by the window and they are playing together once again. And, of course, when she arrived there, Becca licked everyone's face and ears until they were nice and clean.

> I miss you baby,
> Mommy
> Virginia

---

[30] See Barnaby's, Cassidy Sioux's and Sandie's stories elsewhere in the book.

Babies and Bunnies

LITTLE ONE

Little one, little one,
where have you gone?
"To live in the meadow
where summers are long."

Little one, little one,
where do you sleep?
"Beside the still waters,
where God's love runs deep."

Little one, little one,
what do you dream?
"Of licorice and laughter
and saucers of cream."

Little one, little one,
what do you see?
"The prettiest rainbow
that ever could be!"

Little one, little one,
what does it mean?
"That all that is true
doesn't have to be seen!"

- Liz Blackburn

RENATE

Renate died on Good Friday and she was only 2½ years old. She had an adrenal mass, kidney problems, insulinoma, plaque on one of her lungs, and her body was wasting away. She had been a fighter for so long. That week she decided she'd had had enough and passed away in her sleep in our incubator at work. Fortunately, I was with her and had spent my entire Thursday just holding her.

She had stopped eating on Thursday and even refused the food I tried to handfeed her. It broke my heart to force-feed her, but I hoped it would get her interested in eating on her own again. She was lethargic and weak and that evening I knew in my heart that Good Friday would be her last day with us.

I miss her so much; she had become such a big part of my life in such a short time. I put so much time and energy into her care and now I don't know what to do without her. The boys still need me, but not like Renate needed me. Although I miss her so much and cry every day, I know she's not suffering anymore. I think she held on so long just for me. My fiancé said she would not pass away in my arms, but wait until I left her for a few minutes in the incubator to make her peace and then go; this is what she did.

Although Renate was with me for only five short months, I gave her much love and provided her with the best veterinary care available. She was Mommy's pretty girl and I see her everywhere.

> In loving memory of Ren,
> April and Shawn
> Massachusetts

Ferrets will explore anything new in the house. Inspect everything coming into the house, making sure it is totally ferret-proof.

RENNY

Renny would have been 3 years old today, February 24, 2000. She passed away five months ago in September. I still miss her on a daily basis, as much now as ever.

God, if you aren't too busy would you make sure Renny has her thick navy blue ski cap? And could you arrange for her to have some ferret chew toys and chicken and cheese treats? I would be so grateful for your help with my requests, and I know Ren would be, too. Thanks.

I prefer not to think of Renny as my guardian angel because I would much rather be watching over and taking care of her.

Sonya
New Mexico

Keep regular flour (used for baking) handy in case you accidentally cut a toenail a little too much. Dip the nail in a little flour to stop the bleeding. Baking soda or cornstarch will also work to stop a bleeding nail. Next time you are in the pet store, look for KwikStop. It is a powder that will also stop bleeding nails.

ROCKY

My very loveable baby boy, Rocky, passed away today. He was 3 years old. I miss my big boy terribly and wish he was still here. He was buried in a little white casket and inside was the wicker basket he laid in all the time, an afghan and some toys for him to play with in the next world.

I adopted Rocky at the end of September 2001. In October, he was diagnosed with anemia and today we found out he had an egg-sized mass wrapped around his intestines.

I don't understand why this had to happen to my boy. Goodbye my sweet Rocky; your family loves you and misses you very much.

Jessica
Illinois

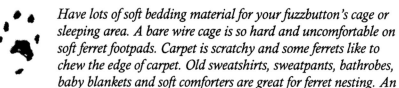

Have lots of soft bedding material for your fuzzbutton's cage or sleeping area. A bare wire cage is so hard and uncomfortable on soft ferret footpads. Carpet is scratchy and some ferrets like to chew the edge of carpet. Old sweatshirts, sweatpants, bathrobes, baby blankets and soft comforters are great for ferret nesting. An adult comforter is too large to fit in a cage, but is great for a large closet in a ferret room. If using a comforter, take extra care to see there are absolutely no holes or ripped seams for curious noses to poke through. If a nose fits in a hole, the ferret body will be next and could end up being a potential casualty. A large comforter can also be cut in two and each piece stitched closed on the cut end, making a smaller comforter that will fit easily inside the closet. This way, you will have a clean spare comforter to use when it is time to change the bedding.

ROCKY

After being diagnosed with lymphosarcoma eight months ago, Rocky finally gave up the battle at 1:15 P.M. on Sunday, July 2, 2000.

About nine months ago, I noticed his right eye appeared swollen and I took him to the vet. The first diagnosis was a simple eye infection. The swelling didn't go away and after a couple of weeks he couldn't close his eyelids. We then set him up for an appointment with an eye specialist. After a few days of waiting for the results, we found out he had a malignant tumor in his head. There wasn't much we could do since it was near his brain.

He still ate and drank fine and acted normal. I lubricated his eyes several times a day since the tumor started pushing on his other eye. Friday night, I noticed that he was lethargic and very weak. We handfed him until I decided not to this morning. When I got him out of his cage this morning, there was no response. I decided not to feed him but to let him go in peace. I placed him in his favorite ferret sleeping bag and laid him on the living room sofa. My 3-year-old son said, "Bye-bye Rocky, you go see Junior now."

Rocky was the famous ferret of *Ferret World* magazine. The photo of him at the keyboard looked like he was actually typing something on the computer. This was not a posed photograph. He was probably trying to get up on the computer desk by grabbing the keyboard and the picture was taken at that moment.

Rocky was almost 7 years old. Goodbye Rock.

Roger
Georgia

ROMEO

Last night when I came home from a long late night at work, my wife told me that the vet called. I could tell before she even told me that it was not good news. Romeo had been through so much. He had both adrenal glands removed and when he had his surgery, he had damage to the vena cava. He had prostate disease and his medication didn't agree with him. After all that, he survived. Earlier this week, Romeo was taken to the emergency clinic when we noticed some bleeding and, sadly, we ended up losing our boy.

I remember when we first brought Romeo home. My wife rushed to pick him up because she thought he was getting ready to poop and he hissed at her. I will remember the cuddling and nap time we had together. I will remember the times he came into the bedroom to wake me up for work. I will remember watching him take his toys out of his toy box and drag them all the way across the house to put them next to my bed. I will remember that he never bit anyone. I will remember the kisses. Romeo was a super ferret and more; I will miss my friend.

Dave
Ohio

 Pieces of heavy cardboard cut to size work well to tape to the bottom of stoves, dishwashers and refrigerators. Kitchen appliances have an area at the bottom where ferrets can crawl in and possibly get stuck behind these items. Thick phone books can be used to wedge between cabinets and appliances or appliances and the wall, wherever there is space. Nail pieces of wood at the bottom of kitchen and bathroom cabinets if there is even the smallest opening. Ferrets are amazingly adept at getting into tiny spaces.

RUSTY

Dear God,
   I have a very heavy heart today. As you know, Rusty passed away last night. He was tucked in his cage last night with his favorite blankie. He lay down on top of it, went to sleep and never woke up. Rusty was about 1.2 pounds when he died. We had tried everything to help him gain weight, but it was no use.
   My husband buried him under a big tree by the house in a box with his blankie and a brass cross. Rusty had a difficult life and we were happy to have him in our lives as long as we did. He finally got to know what being a ferret was all about. He loved talking with the other ferrets in the house, learned to "dook" and enjoy his ferret vitamin treat.
   God, please welcome our Rusty to the Rainbow Bridge. He is a good little guy who will lie in your lap and look up at you with the most loving eyes.

Shelley
New Mexico

Some ferrets sleep so soundly they appear limp and lifeless and it is easy to think they are no longer breathing. Pick them up gently and make sure their body temperature is warm. Feel the stomach and chest area for a regular breathing pattern and heartbeat. Stroke them on the head and shoulders to wake them gently.

RUSTY

Many ferrets rescued from exotic animal auctions are frightened and have been physically abused, not knowing the love and kindness of humans. Rusty was blind in one eye from some type of physical trauma and we can only guess what his life was like before he came to live with us. He didn't let his past stop him from learning to live like a ferret deserves to live. Rusty could tussle with the best of them and he always gently put the other ferrets in their place. He was never a cuddler or a kisser to humans but comforted newcomers and ailing ferrets.

Rusty and I had a special way of showing affection. I would roll up his back end and tussle him and tell him, "I'm getting your butt" and he would dook up a storm. Whenever he'd see me and wanted affection, he'd grab his own butt by rolling up in a ball and placing his front paws behind his back end and he'd dook and roll. Eventually, when I said, "grab your butt," he'd do it right away, tickled at our time of affection.

Each evening Rusty would cruise our home, softly dooking to himself. A few days before he died, Rusty searched out secluded places to sleep, away from the others. I knew even though I couldn't admit it. Even on his last night here in this realm, he wouldn't sleep on my chest. He did sleep in a blanket next to me and I was able to rest my hand gently on his body as he drifted off to sleep, never to awaken.

Rest well my love,
Troy Lynn
Kansas

SAMMY

I had to help my Sammy cross the Rainbow Bridge on November 17, 2001. He was always my big healthy boy until about two weeks ago. It seems adult lymphoma snuck up on us and took him within two weeks of any symptoms. His girlfriend, Nipper, is still here with me, and she's been on medication for almost a year now.

Nipper and I miss Sammy so much. It hurts to lose yet another of my kids, especially so quickly. I know I am blessed to have Nipper[31] still with me to help me get through this difficult time.

Diane
Florida

When your ferret is recuperating from surgery or not feeling well, make sure he/she is eating and drinking enough. Ferrets need plenty of fresh food and water at all times, 24/7. Sometimes ferrets forget to eat and you may have to handfeed them until they are eating again on their own. It is better to feed frequent small amounts rather than one big meal. Ferrets can get dehydrated quickly, especially when sick or vomiting. Occasionally, subcutaneous fluids may have to be administered by your vet, if your ferret is severely dehydrated. Some older ferrets may never eat dry food again and will depend on you for canned or blended food for the rest of their lives.

---

[31] See Nipper's story elsewhere in the book.

SAMSON

A way too young, very skinny and extremely weak baby ferret came into the pet store where I work recently. He had come from a ferret farm. He was unable to eat solid food so I took him home with me to try to get him eating duck soup, etc. He tried very hard for two days but he was just too weak to keep going. I was petting him yesterday and singing to him and telling him what a good boy he was. He was so brave and I am so proud of him. I told him that I knew he was tired and if he was tired of fighting then he could relax and go to sleep. He quit breathing just a few minutes later. I am having him cremated like I plan to do with my own ferrets when they die.

I only knew Samson for two days, but I was so attached to him. He was a beautiful cream color and he was the sweetest boy I have ever met. I will never forget you Sammie. I love you and I miss you so much.

Jennifer
Ohio

Going without food for more than two days can be critical to the health of your ferret. If you are having trouble getting them to eat dry food and they refuse to be handfed softer food, ask a more experienced ferret caretaker for advice or temporary help with your ferret. Consult your veterinarian quickly; you may not have time to wait to see if your ferret gets hungry and decides to eat in a day or two. Take action now.

SANDIE

The last one of the "baby birds"[32] has crossed the Rainbow Bridge. In the spring of 1994, I adopted four adorable ferrets who were sitting snuggled up together in a wicker basket waiting for a new home. They looked like four tiny baby birds waiting to be fed. I decided not to split them up and brought them home to join the other four fuzzies I had at the time.

I named the light colored little boy Sandie because he was the color of beautiful beach sand. Sandie was such a photogenic boy and I have sold many PC mousepads at ferret shows with his picture on it. He had a great personality and got along with all the other ferrets.

Sandie took great delight in dragging his two favorite teddy bears around the house. He would spend endless hours moving them from one place to another.

In January 1999, he had surgery to remove adrenal gland tumors and pancreatic tumors. Although for several months thereafter he enjoyed a good quality of life, his health started failing in the fall. Sandie was 7 to 8 years old when he died on December 18, 1999. He was buried with his favorite teddy bear close beside him.

Coincidentally, three of the four that had been adopted that day in May 1994 died within a few days of Christmas—Barnaby in 1997, Becca in 1998 and Sandie in 1999.

Goodbye my beautiful boy,
Mommy
Virginia

---

[32] See Barnaby's, Cassidy Sioux's and Rebecca Sioux's stories elsewhere in the book.

SASSY

God, my wife and I would appreciate it if you could look out for our baby girl Sassy. She left for the Rainbow Bridge this past week. We would like her to know we love her and hope she is happy. Our baby boy and our other baby girl left us about two years ago and, at that time, we didn't know about The Bridge. All we knew is that they were being well taken of and they were watching down on us.

Please let baby Sassy know we love and miss them all. We will keep wonderful memories of them in our heart. Also, God, please tell Sassy her brothers and sisters miss her very much.

Dennis and Linda
South Carolina

Look for loose threads on towels and blankets used for your ferret's bedding as well as throw rugs (especially those made of nylon or other synthetics) you may have around the house. Toenails can easily get caught in the threads. In trying to free themselves, they may pull out a toenail and hurt themselves or not be able to get loose at all. Cut your ferret's toenails if they are too long, clip loose threads from bedding or, better yet, replace the bedding with another type without threads.

SIMBA

It is with a deep sadness that Simba had to be helped to cross over the Rainbow Bridge yesterday. Simba was my alpha ferret, a sweet albino boy, 7 years old. He was suffering from adrenal disease. Sunday evening I noticed he was having trouble breathing. I held him until midnight and then put him to bed with his two buddies.

Very early the next morning, I awoke and went to check on him. He still wasn't doing well and I brought him upstairs and we lay on the couch together. I hoped he would cross The Bridge on his own. His breathing was labored and it seemed his little heart struggled with every breath. I knew it was time to let my baby go. I could not do anything else for him, except to end his suffering. I held him most of the day and then made a dreaded call to my vet. It was a very difficult decision to make, but at 2:00 P.M., Simba was helped over The Bridge.

God, please look for Simba; he should have arrived yesterday afternoon. He is the sweetest albino who gives kisses to everyone he meets. He has friends who are already there and will be waiting for him. Please let him know that his two brothers looked all over the house for him today, moving their beds, litter box and everything else. I think they wanted to make sure Simba was warm. They snuggled with him continuously during the last few weeks, and it was a comfort to me as well to see them take care of their brother. I told them that Simba will be there, waiting for them, whenever it is their time, and that Simba couldn't possibly eat all the raisins at Rainbow Bridge. I think they are a little worried about that because Simba was such a glutton at treat time.

Some of my friends and family members view pets as animals we keep. Simba was my best buddy, my pal.

Vicki
New York

SKYLER "SKYEBEAR"

I never wanted an albino ferret. When I looked at the translucent red eyes of an albino, it appeared that not only could you look into them, but right through those eyes. It gave me quite a creepy feeling. I've since heard other "ferret people" express the same weird feeling and I still don't understand why we feel this way.

In March 1996 when I adopted Skyler at approximately six months old, he was already a big albino boy. I previously had two dark-eyed white ferrets before, but never an albino. Was I going to accept him or did I still feel a little strange about those eyes? There was no doubt about it; Skyler was a beautiful boy even if he did have those eerie red eyes. Very quickly I grew to love those wonderful red eyes of a ferret who had personality plus. All my furry kids have terrific and distinct personalities, but there was something so special about Skyler that made him stand out in a crowd. I soon starting called him "Big Skye" since he was the biggest boy and it fit him well.

Skyler was always the first ferret up in the morning and he would race out of his room and quickly roll over on his back to have his belly rubbed. He could not start his day until this took place. He loved this ritual, and throughout the day I would stop to give him one more belly rub when he passed my way. Each time I could hear him silently laughing with glee, and I could see such an amazing expression of happiness on his face.

Three years rushed by and in April 1999, at the age of 3½, Skyler was operated on for insulinoma and adrenal tumors. Although the day after surgery he needed a blood transfusion from one of the other furry kids in the household, he began to recover nicely. Three weeks into his recovery, I thought he was certainly out of the woods and was looking forward to a few more years with my precious miniature polar bear. Then I noticed black tarry stools which I knew were a sign of internal bleeding. By the time I could get him to the emergency clinic the next morning, it was too late to save him. On Mother's Day at 8:30 A.M., my Big Skye crossed the

Rainbow Bridge. It is a day I will always remember with great pain and sorrow. Mother's Day will never have the same meaning for me again.

My big SkyeBear, with the beautiful red eyes, was buried in the backyard beside the others who have crossed the Rainbow Bridge before him. There is a note placed in the casket alongside him that says: "This coupon is good for as many belly rubs as you want each day. Love, Mommy, 5/9/99."

> Goodbye my little polar bear,
> Mommy
> Virginia

Recipe for preparing ferret food for sick, old or recuperating ferrets:

- ♥ *Fill a blender half full of water*
- ♥ *Add scoops of your regular dry ferret food and blend well until it is the consistency of thick gravy (you may need to add more water as you add more food)*
- ♥ *Pour the mixture into ice cube trays and put the trays in the freezer*
- ♥ *When the food cubes are thoroughly frozen, remove them from the trays and store them in plastic freezer bags*
- ♥ *At feeding time, remove one cube for each ferret that needs to be fed*
- ♥ *Warm the cube in the microwave or on the stove and add water to make a nice consistency for slurping*

NOTE: *When heating food cubes in the microwave, stir, stir, and stir again before testing the temperature with your finger. Food cooked in the microwave oven gets "hot spots" and you don't want to burn little ferret tongues which are so good for kissing.*

SNOWY

It started Friday night when our 15-month-old Snowy was throwing up. We rushed him to the vet's office and the doctor thought he had a stomach virus. He gave us an antibiotic and said to give him Pepto-Bismol if he was sick again. We left saying we would call on Saturday.

On Saturday Snowy was still not feeling well and, by afternoon, we went back to the vet. He wanted to do blood work. We were up all night with Snowy and he had a difficult night. We continued to give medication.

When I went to discuss the blood work with the doctor on Sunday, Snowy's white count was up and his blood sugar was down, but it still looked like a virus. The doctor said if he stopped eating to get him in immediately, and they would begin giving him some electrolytes. Two hours later, he threw up again and we ran back to the doctor's office. X-rays showed lymphoma in Snowy's chest cavity. Snowy was so sick and there was nothing left to do. My wife and I held him and said our last goodbyes.

This can happen so quickly. Hold your little guys every chance you get, because your time can be so fleeting. Take as many photos as you can. Fortunately, we had just taken new pictures last week.

I know we gave him the very best, but sometimes even that isn't enough. Goodbye Snowy.

John
California

After you drink your half-pint bottle of spring water, roll the bottle on a bare floor and watch the ferrets scramble to play with it. The bottle neck is small enough that a ferret's nose won't fit inside; it makes a wonderful noise as it spins and rolls, and they can grab it with their teeth if the screw top is off. The bottle is very lightweight and can easily be grabbed with both front feet to turn it around and around.

SONNY

Dearest Sonny,
   Thank you for gracing my life. When you came into my life, you were thin and despairing; you looked at me with eyes that broke my heart. I didn't know if you would live the night, let alone extend your six and one-half years. I'm so happy that you decided to stay for awhile and blossom into a sweet trusting ferret that loved to be held on my lap every night while I was at the computer. How much you changed since you first came to me.
   You didn't like it when I put you on a harness and leash to play outside in the grass. Do you remember the elderly Russian couple who spoke no English, but came across the street and wanted to meet you and Sadie and how the woman kept stroking you with obvious delight? What a nice time you gave her. Your dignity amazed me. When I tried to switch you to healthy food, you taught everyone that Meow Mix was number one on the gourmet list. You did gradually learn to eat a healthy diet.
   Last month I found a mass on your left side. I thought it was your spleen and I scheduled a vet appointment. The examination showed it was your kidney, not your spleen, that was affected. Even though you were elderly, the vet suggested exploratory surgery because you seemed so strong. I agreed to it, hoping it would give us more time together. I took you home to coddle and love you for the night. We had a wonderful time at the computer, playing on the floor and watching television together. You ate well and I gave you some cranberry raisins for a treat.
   The next morning, we went to my office again and everyone made a fuss over you. You showed them how charming you were. On the way to the clinic, I set you down in the grass where you sniffed briefly and then looked at me as if to say, "Enough of this, it's cold down here." I carried you in my arms instead, showing you the blooming flowers and the colorful leaves still on the trees. What a beautiful time we had together! At the clinic I kissed you goodbye and reminded you of the Rainbow Bridge and all the friends you would make there while you waited for me.

The afternoon without you was long and I called the vet to check on you before I left the office. They told me your surgery was just starting and I should go home to wait for their call. When I arrived home there were three messages from the clinic. I immediately called the vet who told me he'd found not only a tumor on your kidney, but on your other organs as well. It was virulent and deadly and he couldn't understand how you were still walking around without any symptoms. He asked what I wanted him to do. I told him about our wonderful weekend together and said that rather than put you through the stress of the surgery and watch you die painfully, I wanted to remember how you were those last few days—playing, loving, curious. I asked him to give you a kiss before they ended your life. He said, "I sure will."

I love you little Sonny boy and will forever. Thank you for the memories.

Pat
Pennsylvania

For free ferret toys, save paper and plastic grocery bags. Put several bags on the floor and watch them play for a long time. Cut the handles on plastic bags so there is nothing to trap your ferret. When they crawl through the handle opening, it is possible for the bag to get stuck around their body if the handles are intact. Buy a salad for lunch one day at Wendy's and take the plastic bag home for the ferrets. Ferrets love the crinkly noise of the bag which is very heavy plastic that won't rip. Always supervise your ferrets when playing with plastic bags to avoid any mishaps. Don't let them play in trash bags. These are too large and very hazardous.

SONNY

On Halloween night, Sonny died at the hospital. He came out of surgery and the anesthesia just fine, but the vet suspects that his high temperature was too much for him

I will hate Halloween forever from now on; he was my ray of sunshine. I looked forward to coming downstairs to see him every day. He was so beautiful, so playful, and so happy all the time. He made the others playful. We would just sit here and laugh at him. He looked so sweet when he was sleeping on his back. I thought I was broken in two when Charlie died and thought nothing could be worse, but I was wrong. I have never felt this devastated—Sonny was only six months old.

Sonny is the first ferret we have lost that my husband cried over. I wish I could die. I have nineteen other ferrets, but Sonny was always my favorite

God, why did you have to take Sonny? I have many other ferrets that are sick right now, but you took my youngest, happiest and healthiest; the one who was the light of my life. I have been so down lately, and Sonny was the one bright spot in my day.

Nobody played in this house yesterday; today they played a little. My Sonny is not among them.

Kat
Ohio

Get rid of recliners and sofa beds or put them in a room where the ferrets don't play. Ferrets love to explore inside and underneath these extremely hazardous pieces of furniture. Sometimes ferrets will make their own opening to the inside of furniture if there isn't one already.

SOPHIE

My little girl Sophie, the sweetest of all souls, has gone. I knew this time would come, but that does not make it easier to bear. After over three years of battle against lymphosarcoma and adrenal disease, her heart—enlarged and over worked—finally gave up. Lupron injections had given her back her beautiful coat, but the battle had just exhausted her. She was my "greeting" every day when I got home from work and my constant companion each morning as I got ready to leave again. That much unconditional love should be better rewarded. I hope I will see her again when I cross over. I miss her sweet little face. God, look for Sophie, and tell her my love is unconditional too. The tears won't stop.

J. Stephen
Georgia

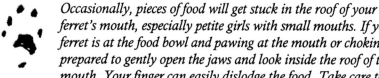

Occasionally, pieces of food will get stuck in the roof of your ferret's mouth, especially petite girls with small mouths. If your ferret is at the food bowl and pawing at the mouth or choking, be prepared to gently open the jaws and look inside the roof of the mouth. Your finger can easily dislodge the food. Take care to remove the food particle completely from the mouth. Hold your ferret upright while removing the food so the particle does not get lodged in the throat.

SQUEEKY AND SNOWBALL

Today was a sad day because we had two ferrets cross over the Rainbow Bridge.

Six-year-old Squeeky, a.k.a. Jaws, was a rescue and a severe biter of males when she came to live with us eighteen months ago. Our retarded daughter managed to turn Squeeky around. Squeeky's insulinoma took us by surprise. We tried medication but it did not work for her because it gave her diarrhea.

Snowball was a 3-year-old who came to us from a bad environment a couple of years ago. He was ill at the time. The ferret room will never be the same because Snowball kept it in a constant uproar. He would not leave the other ferrets alone and never really knew how to play. He went downhill late Saturday night and died early Monday morning.

I picked my wife after work that evening and we went directly to the lumber store with our wood list. Upon arriving home, we started dinner and while it was cooking, we measured, sawed and nailed two pine caskets together. Tomorrow night we will place Squeeky and Snowball in our growing ferret cemetery. There is only silence in the ferret room now and empty cages as they join the four others waiting for them at the Rainbow Bridge. We will greatly miss Squeeky and Snowball.

Harry and Zora Mae
Georgia

 Keep ferrets away from poisons under the sink like dishwashing and laundry detergents.

STEVIE "TEEVEE"

I have never seen a ball bounce halfway up the wall before, especially when being propelled by the tip of a ferret's nose. Stevie could throw a ball or his favorite hollow plastic Easter egg with just a toss of his head. It was as if he were balancing the object momentarily on his nose to achieve just the right trajectory angle before he gave his head the toss. From the very beginning, this was his favorite game and he would amuse himself for hours, tossing and chasing those colored Easter eggs all around the house.

Stevie, or "TeeVee" as I later affectionately called him, was adopted in November 1999 along with Riki, one of his playmates. I couldn't resist either one when I saw them. Stevie was a beautiful albino with gorgeous red eyes and Riki was an amazing chocolate color. When I brought them home, they loved to play together and would frequently get up after all the other ferrets had gone to sleep for the night. They would play a great game of tag by themselves for the longest time. Not only did they entertain each other, but you could see how they both loved interacting with one another. As an observer, I was totally amused as well, even though I had been ready to turn in for the night long ago.

Stevie fit in with the other fifteen ferrets from the very beginning and would play with them, but he continued to be Riki's best buddy.

After Stevie mastered the Easter-egg-up-the-wall trick, he figured out how to open them. He actually made holes with his teeth in the very hard plastic just to get them to open. I would find pieces of colored eggs from time to time hidden in inconspicuous places. It was as if the Easter bunny had dropped a few real eggs from his basket and they had cracked before he had managed to hide them at Easter time.

Each evening when it was time for treats, Stevie was always nearby enough to get to the head of the line. His favorite treats were cucumber and green pepper, which he ate each night. This would make his day complete and he could then go to bed and sleep peacefully.

Stevie found all kinds of things around the house to turn into a game and loved to get his mouth around soda cans and pierce them with his teeth. He would then lick the sweet nectar. He wasn't particular what kind of soda it was, and would break open any and all cans he found. Being in the concession business at the time, I had lots of cases of soda sitting around—at least until I learned that Stevie could empty cans. It often made the carpet very soggy. Once I discovered what he was doing, I had to move the soda cases to another room where he could not get them.

Just before Christmas, I noticed that Stevie was walking around in circles with his head tipped to one side. I took him to the doctor right away and it was thought that he had had a stroke. He was given two medications which did not help. From this moment, Stevie was never the same again. He could not play, climb or even eat by himself. I began feeding him blended ferret food mixed with water and warmed in the microwave. I held him on my lap and hand fed him with a spoon so he would maintain his weight. I had to hold his head still, or at least in the direction of the food bowl, just so he could eat each time I fed him. He was unable to keep his head from rolling back and forth. I was hoping the entire time that he would improve to have some quality of life. I moved him permanently into my room so I could be close, in case he needed me.

Riki didn't understand why Stevie didn't play with him when he tried to start a game of chase or nose tag. Riki had lost his best play buddy.

For a couple weeks, Stevie continued to enjoy his nightly cucumber and green pepper. I watched Stevie get progressively worse and lose more motor control each day. During the second week, he would take a few steps and fall over each time. His body began contorting and he was able to do less and less. After three weeks he could no longer walk, even though he would try. During this time, his mind was still functioning, but his body was failing him. He would attempt to get up to get to the litter box, his legs would move, but his body would twist and turn and he could not stand. It was extremely difficult when I tried to hold him upright in a comfortable position. I was losing him day by day.

I cried lots of tears for Stevie during those three weeks, praying for any improvement in his condition. I cried even more when he died on January 6, 2001. He was laid to rest with several colorful plastic Easter eggs alongside him in the casket so he could bounce them all the way across the Rainbow Bridge.

Of the thirty-four ferrets I've lived with over the past ten years, two of them had the most outgoing and dynamic personality by far than any of the others. One of them was TeeVee and the other is thankfully still with me today. There will never be another ferret with the personality plus of Stevie. He would have been 2 years old in the summer of 2001.

Love,
Mommy
Virginia

Avoid foreign object blockages and huge vet bills for surgical removal of rubber items. Keep erasers, rubber bands, shoes, in-line skates, rubber or latex toys and anything else with rubber on it or in it out of reach. Like a magnet, your ferrets are attracted to and will seek out these items. Once found, the items will quickly be devoured. Some ferrets also like to eat fabric. Check their bedding frequently to make sure there are no holes from chewing on it.

STINKY

Stinky was our first ferret and held a special place in our hearts. He was smart as a whip to boot. We paid $150 to rescue him from a bad situation and he was worth every penny and more. He was my best friend and companion for seven and one-half years. He was a great public relations ferret who was loved by many people. He liked to meet the public and helped teach basic ferret care classes.

Stinky was generally a healthy ferret until he got older when he got several diseases that afflict all fuzzies. Stinky and I went through many ups and downs since October 2001. I tried everything I could to help him. Stinky was helped to cross over The Bridge on Friday afternoon, March 8, 2002. Although I am very sad, I am happy knowing he will never feel pain again and that he is running and playing with brothers, sisters and friends waiting at The Bridge. Stinky was 8 years old and did not run and play anymore because he had a heart condition.

Stinky, you will always be loved.

Donna
New Jersey

 Attach all floor register covers over the securely with screws so you don't have to tear apart the heating ducts to find lost ferrets that fell through a hole in the floor. Ferrets are smart enough and strong enough to remove covers that are not securely fastened.

SURABI

This afternoon, my eldest ferret, Surabi, crossed the Rainbow Bridge. I know she never met my dogs because they all passed before she came to live here. But I can imagine Daisy, my little poodle mix, greeting her. She and Surabi had so much in common—both were rescued from an abusive environment to be loved and pampered by me, both lived to a very old age and both slowly went blind. Daisy passed two months before Surabi came into my life and from the beginning I could sense the similarities in their personalities. I try to imagine them waiting for me together. I know Daisy had my previous dogs there to greet her at The Bridge and I'd hate to think Surabi had no one.

Last night, I held and cuddled my little girl, Surabi, cooing to her and trying to get her to drink some water. She lay so still and quiet in my arms and I had the terrible feeling this was goodbye.

This morning, when I checked on her she was asleep, curled up with my other two girls. This afternoon, when I opened the cage to let them spend the rest of the day romping, Surabi had already left for the Rainbow Bridge. She hadn't moved from where I had seen her earlier in the day and still lay with her two sisters, who kept looking around and wondering where their sister was hiding. Even the cat seems to know she's missing.

I went outside in my despair and through my tears used a pickaxe to chop through the frozen ground. I wrapped Surabi in her favorite blanket and put her in a little box. She was laid to rest near Daisy's burial site.

Rhoni
Pennsylvania

SWEET AMADEUS VAN GOGH

Amadeus was my first rescue. When I first saw him, he was standing attentively in his cage and I fell in love immediately. Although he was deaf and needed special handling to stop his biting, we worked it out. We became incredibly close and he would often crawl on my lap as I sat at the computer. At shows, people would do a double take when they saw Amadeus asleep in one of my arms and Shiloh in the other. I enjoyed putting Ami in people's arms to watch their eyes soften and have them say, "Gee, I wish I had a ferret I could cuddle." He was my dearest boy and I'll always remember the torn ear that changed his name to "Sweet Amadeus van Gogh."

Today my heart is breaking—I've just returned home from taking Amadeus to the clinic, where I assisted him on his way to the Rainbow Bridge. I planned to take him last night, but I couldn't find a ride. This turned out to be a blessing. Amadeus was on medication and wasn't suffering; he was just very weak and sleepy. With the reprieve I set about making it a day of treasured memories. We watched television and slept together last night. I woke early this morning, stroked him gently and smothered his sweet face with kisses until the alarm went off. He seemed to like this. I was trying to save up memories for when he wasn't around anymore.

Amadeus crawled out of the cuddle sack I had been carrying him around in and drank endlessly from the dog's water bowl. Once I got dressed and ready for work, I picked him and the sack up and took him to work with me. Several people stopped by to cuddle him and offer their sympathy. Everyone was supportive of my decision, which was very helpful. A coworker gave Ami some Cheerios which he happily ate. He ate about a tablespoon of baby food and lapped up an unbelievable amount of diet soda. On the day you are going make the journey to The Bridge; it is okay to eat junk food, isn't it? After work, I took Amadeus and the dog to the park. Today, Ami felt too sick to enjoy digging in the dirt or playing in the sand pit.

Too soon, I was heading for the vet's office. When I arrived, I was ushered into a waiting room where a technician gave Amadeus a sedative. The doctor and I talked about how quickly the cardiomyopathy had taken Ami and how puzzled I was that he never coughed. The doctor said that in most cases he's seen, a ferret doesn't develop a cough, but just takes an incredibly fast decline like Amadeus did. I'm glad the disease was not prolonged because watching him fail over a longer period would have been heart breaking.

I'll cherish the times we spent wrestling, walking in the woods and wooing people with his sweet nature. I was blessed with his presence for 3½ of his 4¾ years. Of course I wanted more time with him, but I am still in awe at how much I received from our time together. Please wait for me at The Bridge my Sweet Amadeus so I can to scoop you up, smother you with kisses once again and let you show me how much you missed me (OUCH!).

I miss you with all my heart,
Your loving mama
Pennsylvania

Have an evacuation plan in case of emergencies. If your ferrets have their own room, have small cages for sleeping and, if necessary, putting ferrets in to carry quickly outside. If your ferrets sleep in a large closed cage, have a couple of strong pillowcases within easy reach to put ferrets in to get to safety. You can easily make a stronger pillowcase sack for carrying several ferrets to temporary shelter. Just buy two yards of 45" quilted fabric at the fabric store. Fold the material in half on the longest side and stitch one long side and one short side, leaving one short side open. The fold will be on one of the long sides. Hem the raw edges of the opening for a more finished sack. Put the sack on a shelf near the ferret's sleeping area so you can grab it quickly if an emergency arises.

SWEETIE

Today, very briefly, I met a little girl named Sweetie. Sweetie's momma knew she was very ill, and needed to go to The Bridge. But her momma couldn't stay with her because it was too painful for her. Her momma said goodbye and told Sweetie she would miss her very much.

I was working at the clinic today and was there when Sweetie came in. I held her and told her about The Bridge and how she would be well again. I let her know it was all right, that her momma loved her so much she brought her to us so we could show her the way to The Bridge. She nuzzled my fingers and my hand to let me know she understood. I could tell she was so tired and needed to go home. The vet then helped Sweetie find her way home. I held her until she was gone; telling her how nice The Bridge was, that she would meet friends and could wait there for her momma.

God, Sweetie has a friend there, but I don't know her name; maybe you know who she is. Sweetie's a little sable. Let her know how much she was loved and that she will be missed, would you? Tell her I felt honored to hold her and to be able to tell her about The Bridge.

Rebecca
Indiana

Think about acupuncture therapy to treat many ferret conditions. Talk to an experienced acupuncturist to find someone familiar with treating animals. See Jakob's story of The Acupuncture Treatment in the appendix.

Fuzzbean Crossing

It's So Tasty

A TIDY HOUSE

There are no messes anymore;
No misplaced poopies on the floor,

No litter that I need to sweep,
no "shower tracks" of little feet,

No medicines to measure now,
and no more need to worry how.

The basket in the bathroom stands
untipped by little fuzzy hands,

There's no one here to knock it down;
no little furry, fuzzy clown.

The house is tidy once again,
without my little messy friend,

I miss the messes that he made,
and wish so much he could have stayed.

Our house is tidy; wood and stone,
but now this house is half a home.

- Liz Blackburn

TASHA

Tasha was quietly sent on to The Rainbow Bridge this afternoon. She had cancer, and the vet and I both agreed it was time to let her go. Tasha was a tiny ferret on the outside, but her heart was one of the biggest I've had the pleasure to meet. She loved her tennis ball and would drag it backward around the room. She taught all the other ferrets how to walk a plastic bag from the inside.

Tasha got along with all the animals—cats and ferrets and was even very kind to the ailing senior family cat. She taught me that grace is possible, even when you're hurting. I'll miss you little ferret girl. I hope you have all your fur back now and your friends are dancing with you.

Sandy
New Mexico

Try bathing your ferrets while you shower. Hold them in your arms instead of letting them run around the tub. A ferret's body temperature is a few degrees warmer than ours (100°-103°) and they enjoy comfortably warm water. Once they are sufficiently wet, lather them with a mild pet shampoo. Gently rinse them under the showerhead to remove all the soap. Try not to get soap or water directly in their face or eyes. Have a towel handy next to the shower so you can grab it easily and quickly. Towel off the ferret a little, if they will let you, and put them on the floor with the towel to let them continue drying themselves. Keep the bathroom door closed so they will have a warm room and won't get chilled while they are wet. Finish your shower and make sure the ferret is almost dry before letting them out of the bathroom. After bathing, it's the perfect time to clean cute little ferret ears. NOTE: Invest in a showerhead with one hundred or more fine holes for a very gentle and comfortable shower for you and your ferret.

TASHA

Dear God,
   This is the second time in less than a week I'm asking for your help. Our little foster ferret, Tasha, had to be helped to The Bridge this evening. We had her such a short time. Although we don't know how old she was, she was rather elderly and such a sweet loveable little girl. When I held her, she was very content to just lay there and sleep. She loved to gather plastic grocery bags and drag them into a paper grocery bag where she would curl up in her newly made nest and sleep. If possible, could you find her some bags up there?
   And, God, would you introduce her to the others waiting there for her. Tasha is bringing some Kix to share with all her family, even though she didn't know most of them. We miss her so much, as we do all the rest. Tell her we love her and we are so glad we were able to give her a loving home the last few months of her life.
   God, it helps to ease our pain to know you will help Tasha settle in. Thank you.

Mary Jo
Arizona

 Watch expiration dates on your ferret's medication. Make sure all meds are fresh and not outdated. Many medications need to kept in the refrigerator. Ask your vet which ones to refrigerate.

TASSIE

Our baby, Tassie, left us on Sunday, June 10, 2001. She was a little over 4 years old.

Tassie, short for Tasselhoff Burrfoot, joined our family with her brother four years ago. When picking them out from the happy, wiggling mass at the pet store, I did the diplomatic thing. I stuck my hand into the aquarium and Tassie climbed over her littermates and clung to my arm. Such tactics were typical of her. We called Tassie our "cinnamon girl" because her coat had an auburn tint.

Tassie was the craftiest little female I've ever met, especially if it involved getting to a soda can. When she appeared with dirt on her nose and feet one day, we were stunned to realize she'd been in a plant that was on a little stand. She had managed to get herself between the bookcase and the stand, pushed her back against the bookcase and walked up the side of it, like a scene from Mission Impossible. You never knew when you were going to see Tassie's face poking out of a kitchen drawer she was hiding in.

Tassie loved to play with squeaky dog toys; the Evil Spider was her favorite. Whenever she heard a squeaky toy, she would wake from a dead sleep. When she and her sister did the Great Ferret Escape two years ago, Tassie appeared sitting somewhat impatiently on her hind feet with her little arms stretched up, wanting the squeaky toy that had been used to lure them back.

Tassie had successful adrenal surgery in the fall and was happy, healthy, and spoiled. A few months later, Tassie became ill again and it quickly turned to critical. She was taken to the vet and an x-ray showed she had fluid around her heart; her lungs and heart were failing.

On Sunday morning, she was gone; it had happened quickly. Tassie is our second loss and the grief we feel is immense. There is so much pain, guilt and anger that there were no warnings until it was too late.

Julie
Ohio

TAWNEE SIOUX

She was so wicked right from the start. A nasty little ferret girl, all one and one-half pounds of her. I probably should have had some indication of her temperament when I saw her hanging off the lip of the breeder's son when he held her a little too close to his face. At the time she was just a few weeks old, even too young to bring home with me.

When I lost my first little girl ferret, I was left with only one boy. I knew I wanted another little girl to replace the one I had lost and to be a companion to the remaining ferret. I went to a breeder who lived nearby, to see if she had any ferrets for sale. She had a litter that had been born a few weeks earlier. When I looked at them, I saw the smallest little sable girl who was a beautiful tawny brown color. I fell in love with her immediately and decided to purchase her. I could not bring her home for several more weeks, however, because she was not old enough to leave her mother. I had already decided on a perfect name for her—Tawnee Sioux. Her middle name was in memory of Demi Sioux, the first little girl ferret I lost. From then on, all my girls have been given the same middle name.

I thought about Tawnee Sioux for days and could hardly wait for the next few weeks to pass until I could bring her home. When she was eleven weeks old, I finally picked her up from the breeder. Right from the start Tawnee didn't like me, and that's putting it mildly. Although she weighed only a few ounces, she attacked me viciously on several occasions and I'm convinced she wanted to kill me and drag me away. She tried that, too. One day she bit the flesh off the end of my big toe, which managed to bleed all over the carpet once it completed soaked through my sock. Then she tried to drag me forcefully across the room. I was almost ready to give her back to the breeder after a few days of this behavior. I decided against it, however, and thought I would work with her, and hopefully be able to modify this horrible behavior. How could this little tiny ball of fur be so nasty?

Two months later, I was given another little girl named Mistie Sioux. When Mistie came to live with us, Tawnee tried to kill her too. Each day I had to put a plastic milk crate upside down over Tawnee so she was in a mobile cage. As tiny as she was, she was so strong she pushed that milk crate all over the house. It's difficult to remember when Tawnee's behavior changed for the better, if it ever did. She did mellow after some months, but continued to be aggressive to all newcomers, even at her tiny size. At her heaviest, she was no more than one pound and ten ounces.

A few years ago, Tawnee finally slowed down a bit due to her advancing age. She had adrenal tumors removed as well as insulinoma and part of her tail amputated because of a tumor. She continued to be in good health for the rest of her life. The last year, she slept most of the time and had no interest in playing with the new kids, who were much too active for her. She would only get up late at night when the other ferrets had gone to sleep already. She only ate food I had processed in the blender and warmed in the microwave and she was on daily medication.

Three days after one of my other ferrets died, I noticed Tawnee was not doing well. When I had her checked, the doctor said she had congestive heart failure. She lived two more days but her heart was just too old and it was working so hard.

Unlike the way she started in the world back in 1993, Tawnee Sioux left quietly on February 11, 2001. She would have been 8 years old on August 30. Her life was long and I'm thankful that my time with her was also.

Missing my feisty little girl,
Mom
Virginia

THELMA

They say bad things happen in threes, I certainly hope I have had my fill. Last Easter, I had to help two of my ferrets cross the Rainbow Bridge. Two months ago, Thelma (yes, she does have a sister Louise) went in for exploratory surgery. She was diagnosed with inflamed bowels, was treated for this, and all was well. Within two to three weeks after surgery, she sounded like she had a cold and was given an antibiotic, which did not help her condition. She then had an x-ray which showed an enlarged heart and fluid in her lungs. She was treated with more medication and, unfortunately, got worse. There was nothing that I could do to help her. I went to the hospital, held my sweet little girl in my arms and released her from her pain and suffering. Thelma was only 2 years old.

I rescued Thelma and her sister from a pet store when they were nine months old. The two of them were hellions. They had been kept in a pet store for eight months, getting poked and prodded constantly. They bit and drew blood like there was no tomorrow. After I brought them home, they were running around the apartment and even though I knew they were biters, I was in bare feet. Thelma saw flesh and tore after me as I ran down the hallway and jumped upon my bed. Here I am, standing on my bed thinking, "this is cute." I run a shelter, I pride myself on having rehabilitated several biters, and I am hiding from this fuzzy who probably weighs two pounds. Needless to say, after four or five months, both Thelma and her sister came around. I continued to be the only one who could handle either of them without getting bit.

Thelma gave me a new perspective on life. She was an aggressive ferret, but once she learned to trust me, she gave herself to me completely. I will never forget when the day came that I could hold her and she no longer bit me. That feeling of accomplishment and bonding is one I will never forget.

God, please put Thelma in your thoughts tonight, she was way too young to cross The Bridge. I know she is with her two brothers who loved her very much. And, God, even though I know

Fuzzbean Crossing

I tried everything I could, I wish there was something else I could have done to help her live a longer and happier life.

Marion
Ontario, Canada

Ferrets have a habit of wiping their chin on the rug after eating. Some even wash their face and hands in the water bowl before eating. Be prepared to clean up spilled water that has splashed out of the bowl. Some ferrets like to stand or swim in the water bowl, some like to splash water out of the bowl and some like to drag the bowl around. Try placing a small towel under the water bowl for catching any spills. At least your floor will be clean from all the splashed water you've wiped up.

TIA

This morning, Tia, our oldest and first ferret, passed away in her sleep. She was a great ferret ambassador and would quickly win over, "ieeww, what's that, a rat?" people. She was always small, which made her even cuter and more endearing. She was sweet, never nipped, and always found the litter box.

When Tia was young, she used to perform the most amazing and unbelievable feats like shelf-climbing and pocketbook opening.

We lay her in a box this morning along with her collar, a small blanket and her favorite toy. Each of the other ferrets gave her kisses on the ears. Even one of our cats came and patted Tia on the head with his paw.

Tia had a partial pancreaotomy well over a year ago, and beat the average by three months. That was just like her to be a little more determined. She was the main reason we have four other fuzzies. We loved her dearly and miss her terribly.

Sadly,
Mark and Midge
Pennsylvania

Never have your ferret declawed. This is painful and unnatural. Ferrets need their claws to scratch themselves, dig in the litter box and climb. Without claws, they will be unable to do the things that ferrets do naturally.

TINY

Dear God,
    Please welcome Tiny; he passed over The Bridge tonight. He is just a very little guy and is going to miss his brothers. He tried very hard these last two weeks, but lost the battle today. He will be looking for his buddy who passed over The Bridge two years ago. He was very small but had a very big heart. He will be always remembered and missed by his Mom and brothers. Goodnight Tiny, we love you.

                                        Mom

P.S. He loves raisins

Consider herbal remedies for treating various ferret conditions. Do some research on herbs by getting a good herb book and talk to an herbalist before administering any herbs on your own. Herbs are very powerful and it only takes a few drops to treat a small animal like a ferret. Treating with herbs is not a quick fix for an ailing ferret but rather an alternative to work synergistically with "Western" medications. Herbal therapy may be a solution when there are no other options available.

TOOTLES

Dear God,
   My grandson, Donald, asked me to ask you to look for his beloved ferret, Tootles, who went to the Rainbow Bridge about a year ago. He might be with my beloved Scruffy. He would like Tootles to know he still loves him and misses him. Donald would like to know how Tootles is doing and what his favorite activities are. Donald looks forward to an answer at your earliest convenience, because he knows just how busy you are, God.

Rev. Ron
Michigan

 If using an ear cleaning solution for rinsing your ferret's ears, warm the solution container (usually plastic bottle) in a bowl of warm water first. This way you are not putting very cold liquid into your ferret's ears which is extremely uncomfortable. Test the ear cleaning solution container before using it to make sure it is just comfortably warm, not too cold or not too hot.

TUCKER

On December 17, 1999, my shelter Mom got in a bunch of ferrets rescued from a backyard breeder. I picked out a sweet little dark-eyed white/sterling silver unaltered male. I named him Tucker and brought him home December 19. He was approximately 2½ years old and horribly thin from a diet of generic cat food. His hind legs had atrophied from being kept in a two-foot square breeding cage. He wasn't allowed out of the cage to play and he had no social interaction with humans. Oddly enough he didn't bite.

I brought him home and turned him loose in the apartment. I already had four ferrets and I knew it was safe enough for a sick little guy like him to explore. Oh, the dooking; he was convinced he was in heaven. He found the water bowl and tried to take a bite out of the water. I think he had never drunk water from a bowl before. I laughed myself silly watching him try to figure out how to get the water out of the bowl and into his mouth without dunking his nose in it. Quickly, he figured it out. The first night, I kept him in a crate apart from the others and he had a selection of several foods from which to choose. He didn't eat a lot but he sampled everything. Since he was eating and drinking well, I thought he was doing as well as could be expected. We did introductions the next day with the other ferrets, since everyone came from the same shelter and had been exposed to the same things. Tucker and my two albinos became a threesome almost immediately. They taught him to play follow the leader and how to hide from Mom. They did all they could do to make him feel welcome, including curling up with him.

I was aware of his hind leg weakness but thought it was the atrophy that made him fall. I also noticed he was grinding his teeth, which I thought was a tummy ache from the traveler's diarrhea and shelter shock. I treated him with Pepto-Bismol and Kaopectate[33].

---

[33] ¼ teaspoon as needed for diarrhea or upset stomach.

Since Tucker seemed to be improving each day, I wasn't terribly concerned about the amount of time he spent sleeping. I thought he was just weak from all that he'd been through. I was so wrong. I found him in a coma about 3:00 P.M. and rushed him to my shelter Mom. He passed away in my arms at 6:05 P.M. Christmas day, right after I kissed him goodbye between the ears. We did all we could for him, but the insulinoma was far too advanced and he never came out of the coma.

When I think back on the time I had with him, I can't help but smile through the tears. For those seven days, the last seven days of his life, he was happy. He had all he wanted to eat and he was rarely caged. He slept so much; you didn't even know he was there. I could find him easily in the same box of clothes in my closet, scoop him up and put him in a fleece snuggle sack. I would then hold him for as long as he was willing to stay in my lap. He had friends to play with for the first time in his life and he was loved.

Despite the pain I'm feeling, I also feel a lot of joy and don't regret adopting him for one single moment. I thanked my shelter Mom for letting me have the time with such a sweet, wonderful and loving ferret. I am thankful I got to be the one to make Tucker's last few days happy.

                                          Erin
                                        Washington

Female ferrets need to be spayed at about 6 months of age. If you purchased your ferret at a pet store, most likely this has already been done. If your ferret came from a breeder, ask the breeder if spaying has been done already. If female ferrets are not spayed or bred, they may develop anemia and die.

TUCKER

On March 15, 2001, the doctor examined Tucker and said he had insulinoma and there was nothing that could be done for him. I took Tucker back home because I thought he would be more comfortable there than in the hospital. Two hours later, Tucker went into screaming seizures, which made my Mom panicky. I held Tucker close and had my Mom take me back to the vet. I couldn't bear to see my baby go through another seizure and had the vet help him cross the Rainbow Bridge.

Even today when I think about him, I still cry because it is so difficult to lose your first ferret. I am so angry because they don't deserve to die so soon.

Buffie
Texas

For more free ferret toys, go to the local home improvement center or carpet store and ask for an empty carpet tube. Cut off the ends of the tubes because they have plastic inserts that are difficult to remove. Then cut the tubes in half and you will have two heavy duty ferret tunnels approximately 5½ feet long.

TYSON

My beloved Tyson passed on to The Bridge on Monday, June 24, 2002. It happened so suddenly. He was not doing well the morning of June 17, and I took him to the vet. He was fine the night before—eating and drinking and then sleeping in his favorite hidey place in the foyer. I don't know how he got sick so fast. The vet said he had a bad case of gingivitis and prescribed Clavamox[34]. I took him home, mashed his food up, and gave him his medications. He was doing better on the third day, but he was losing weight fast. I tried the gravy recipes which he liked. He was drinking and urinating and, therefore, I was not worried about dehydration. On June 24, Tyson had a seizure and was so weak he couldn't hold his head up. I gathered him in my arms and took him to the vet. Tyson was too weak and too old to make it through the rest of the day. I said my goodbyes, and stood with him while the vet gave him the shot to end all pain on this earthly realm. My Tyson was gone, my little gray-haired cuddle bunny.

Tyson was a throw away; the woman who gave him up no longer wanted him. He had bitten off her guinea pig's ear and, hence, the name Tyson stuck with him. He did not like other ferrets and quickly let them know that he would not engage in their silly war dancing antics. He claimed a big forest green sleep sack for his personal domain, and the other ferrets soon learned to steer clear of him. Even my black-eyed-white, the feistiest and nuttiest ferret, respected Tyson's need for solitude. With me, Tyson was the most loving ferret I have known. He would take naps with me, crawl into bed with me at night, and sleep nestled in a ball against the small of my back. He showered me with kisses, and loved sharing broiled chicken with me. He was amazing in so many ways. I estimated him at about 6 to 7 years of age. Tyson was very picky with his choice of raisins and preferred only the plumpest and juiciest ones in the can. And they absolutely had to be California raisins in the red canister.

---

[34] See the appendix for a description of this medication.

Fuzzbean Crossing

I still have thirteen other little devils to love and help me make it through all this. They still go near Tyson's giant green sleep sack and look, but I think they know he is gone. It hurts so much to lose these little guys.

> Diane
> Arkansas

Male ferrets should be neutered to prevent excessive fighting with other male ferrets. If you purchased your ferret at a pet store, neutering was probably already done. Ask the pet store or the breeder where you purchased your ferret about the neutering.
Ferrets will fight amongst themselves on a day-to-day basis and neutering will not alleviate this. They are territorial creatures and will quarrel over sleeping areas, food, treats or a new ferret in the household. This is normal behavior. Unaltered males, on the other hand, can become so aggressive they can hurt or even kill another male. Males that have not been neutered will also have an extremely strong odor.

WANDA

I had to have my sweet little Wanda put to sleep today. She had been sick for two months and no vet could determine what was wrong with her. Even these ferret-knowledgeable vets were stumped. Wanda got better for awhile, but this weekend she went downhill. Her back legs got so weak; she could barely get up to go to the bathroom. I made the decision on Sunday to help her pass on. I know she is happy and no longer in pain. Her Daddy and I are so very sad. God, could you please watch over her. She is a little sable girl who loves to steal socks and eat peanut butter. I will love her forever. Her brothers and sister miss her greatly.

Jaki
Virginia

When cleaning ferret rooms, bathrooms, or any place that ferrets walk, do not use Lysol unless you rinse it away completely and dry the area thoroughly afterward. This cleaner is toxic to your fuzzballs. Use extreme caution when using store-bought cleaners of any kind. Better yet, make your own cleaners with common household ingredients. Keep a spray bottle of household vinegar handy for quick cleanups and disinfecting ferret areas. Use apple cider or other vinegar that indicates 5 percent strength on the back of the bottle. Find a great website for homemade cleaners in the appendix.

WARLOCK

"They're so adorable," I said to my son about the two white fuzzballs in the cage. Each time I saw them, their little pink noses were pressed against the bars of the cage, just wanting to be let out. My son felt he no longer had the time necessary to spend with them. At the time I knew nothing about ferrets—their needs, habits, care or feeding—but said I would take them home to live with me and the two cats. I had no idea at the time what a drastic change these little balls of fur would bring to my life.

I soon realized what personality these small creatures had and what care they required. Over the weeks, I learned they needed interaction with me and should not be left alone in a cage to sleep by themselves. They enjoyed each other immensely, entwining their bodies around each other in sleep. When awake, they ran, chased each other, and explored during their playtime.

When the ferret girl died of insulinoma shortly over a year later, Warlock was left alone and I adopted another ferret a few days later to be his companion. They got along with each other immediately. I learned later this was not always the case when a new adoptee arrives. Over the next two years, several more furries were adopted and they all loved Warlock. Warlock was truly the alpha ferret in the bunch. I'm not sure if this was due to the fact that he was the first ferret in the household. He was "The Fonz" of ferretdom—totally cool. He never once became aggressive toward another ferret and loved to play with them all, especially his buddy Koti.

A new ferret I adopted brought ECE[35] into the household and Warlock got very sick and almost died. After spending a week in the hospital, he returned home in worse condition than when he had arrived. He was unable to stand and had lost a lot of weight. I was determined I was not going to lose another fuzzy so soon after I had lost the first one. I managed to nurse Warlock back to health by feeding him every two hours around the clock. After one week of hand feeding, he began to show some interest in eating and

---

[35] See Epizootic Catarrhal Enteritis in the appendix.

drinking again on his own. He slowly gained the weight back that he had lost with the virus, but it took several months before he was back to his normal weight.

In January 1996, I noticed he was losing weight again and I became concerned. Although he was eating and drinking and his stools were normal, something was wrong. Warlock came down with diarrhea the last week in January and I took him in for a checkup. When the doctor felt Warlock's abdomen, he said he could feel cancer spread throughout his body and felt surgery would be of no use. I took him home to make him comfortable and watch for signs of sickness and degeneration.

Warlock was a 5-year-old black-eyed white ferret who crossed his hands when he slept as if he were saying his prayers. Most of the time he would sleep by himself, but occasionally enjoyed the company of others curled up close to him. Each new ferret adoptee loved Warlock and never attempted to fight or antagonize him. On one occasion, another adoptee thought he wanted to be the dominant ferret, but Warlock quickly pinned him to the floor. There was no fighting and it happened very quietly. This only happened once and the new ferret understood that Warlock was in charge. There was never another confrontation after this.

Warlock's favorite treats were strawberries, bananas and peanut butter. I could never eat an ice cream sandwich without having him on my lap helping me devour it. I think he would have eaten the entire thing if I had let him, but he only got a very small taste. He was such a joy and could roll over better than a trained dog, even though I never taught him to do this. He had great strength in his legs and loved to kick the pillows off the couch onto the floor.

On Wednesday, February 7, when I got up in the morning Warlock was making strange noises with his mouth open. I rushed him to the doctor who said he was gasping for air and near death. He was given an injection to avoid any further suffering. At 12 o'clock noon, five days after his buddy Koti left us, Warlock joined him across the Rainbow Bridge. One short week after Warlock had been diagnosed with cancer, he was gone. Thankfully, he did not seem to be in pain or be suffering from anything except diarrhea for the last few days.

Fuzzbean Crossing

I am heartbroken my beautiful boy has gone, but we will all survive somehow knowing that he lived a good and happy life. It isn't the same without him here, but at least Koti isn't alone any more. I know he has his little hands crossed and is saying his prayers up in heaven. I love you and goodbye my little "leader of them all."

Mommy
Virginia

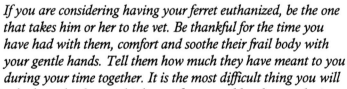 *If you are considering having your ferret euthanized, be the one that takes him or her to the vet. Be thankful for the time you have had with them, comfort and soothe their frail body with your gentle hands. Tell them how much they have meant to you during your time together. It is the most difficult thing you will ever have to do, but who do you think your ferret would rather see during their last few moments of life—the one who has cared for them and loved them or someone else?*

WHISKEY SOUR

Whiskey Sour was a breeder ferret, born in 1996, who came to our shelter almost two years ago. He was a panda ferret who came for intensive rehabilitation because he was a bad biter. Immediately, upon leaving his carrier, he decided my nine-year-old daughter was his soulmate. He climbed into her arms, gripped her finger with his paw and went to sleep. So it was that Whiskey came here to live with us permanently.

My daughter didn't like the name Whiskey, so she called him Whiskers. Whiskers had a great life; he played every day, had lots of love and attention and ate good food. I think he was happy here, and he certainly loved his best friend.

Yesterday, we noticed his eye and his belly were swollen. We took him to the vet and he was given antibiotics. My daughter sat up with him all that night offering him baby food, duck soup and water every hour; but it was not to be. At 10:30 A.M. today, Whiskers passed on to The Bridge in the arms of his soulmate. His paw was wrapped around her finger, the same way it was when he chose her.

My daughter is grief stricken and the other ferrets can't seem to figure out where their hammock warmer is. I know he is happy and out of pain now.

God, can you be on the lookout for a panda ferret? He could never seem to get the hang of war dancing down here so maybe you could set him up with a teacher there. Let Whiskers know that his soulmate cries constantly and his brothers and sisters miss him. His Mama wishes she could have saved him. We all loved him so deeply, always and forever.

Marta
Arkansas

WHITE RUSSIAN

On May 8, 2002, less than one week after his son had to be helped to the Rainbow Bridge, White Russian lost his two-year fight against Aleutian disease[36]. Months ago, Russian developed heart and respiratory problems which had been controlled with medication. For the past few weeks, he also had four daily nebulizer treatments. On May 7, he was not responding well to those treatments. The next day, he went into respiratory distress and treatments only helped for a few minutes. He was unable to get comfortable and got up every few minutes, wheezing, gagging and choking. The vet, who had been treating Russian's symptoms for almost two years, met me at the clinic and felt that there was nothing we could do for him once the nebulizer no longer helped.

Russian had again been very aggressive towards his cagemates the last few weeks and had to be separated from them. He was up a lot during the night, angrily knocking litter boxes out of his way, obviously in a rage. Many nights he didn't sleep much. I gave him some pain medication before we left for the vet's office, and he soon gave a sigh and lost the tension that had become a part of his life. He again became the calm sweet boy he had been most of the time. In my heart I knew what was coming, and I held him close and spoke to him about the Rainbow Bridge. I told him he would see his best friend again. I told him how much I loved him and what an impact his life has had, making people care about Aleutian disease. At the vet's office, Russian kissed me goodbye. It was so incredibly hard not to just run out the door to take him home again.

Judy
Illinois

---

[36] There is a simple test for Aleutian disease that can be performed at home or by your veterinarian.

WHITE RUSSIAN

Today is a very hard day for me. I heard that my hero, White Russian, died.[37] I can't begin to tell you how deeply this affects me and how I feel right now.

I first saw White Russian when I was surfing on the Internet. I've never seen anything like him before or since. He looked like a fluffy panda bear with a great spark in his eye and a mouth that looked like he was smiling. And what striking markings he had. His Mom, Judy, told me he was from an Australian/New Zealand line of spunky ferrets. He was a gentle giant, full of love and life.

I later found out that Russian had contracted Aleutian disease, known as ADV,[38] and his time here was limited. There is currently no cure for this contagious disease. How could God let this disease strike such a magnificent angel? I believe Russian's reason for being here was to make people aware of ADV and inspire them to fight this awful disease. Why was I having such a hard time saying goodbye to him? I think it is because he is a legend and legends don't die; there is no goodbye for me. Russian, I'll look for you in heaven when I get there so I can see your smile once again.

Rebecca
Tennessee

Ferrets are in the same family as weasels, mink, skunks and otters. Like skunks, ferrets can spray when attacked or frightened. However, unlike skunks the ferret odor is not strong and it dissipates very quickly. You will be aware that your ferret has sprayed a scent but it will not be objectionable. If you purchased your ferret from a pet store, they probably have already been surgically descented.

---

[37] See the story on the previous page.
[38] Look for more information on this disease in the appendix.

WINNIE

Winnie had surgery a few years ago for insulinoma and adrenal disease and, up until recently, was doing well. I took her to the hospital Saturday morning because she had a wheezing hacking cough which I thought was a hairball problem. But it wasn't a hairball, Winnie had congestive heart failure. I took her home, along with some medication.

Later that day, Winnie had a bad hypoglycemic episode. I rushed her to the twenty-four-hour emergency hospital. She was hypoglycemic and hypothermic. The doctor warmed her up in a tiny incubator and managed to get her blood sugar level up. I took her home again, waking up during the night to feed her and give her water. She was doing well the next day. I woke her up in the afternoon to give her some water from a syringe, but she had stopped breathing and her heart had stopped.

I had been a paramedic for eight years, but never thought I'd be doing CPR on my own ferret. I brought her around to where she had a weak pulse. I rushed her again to the hospital and, after talking to my veterinarian, decided it was time to help her cross over the Rainbow Bridge. It was the hardest thing I've ever had to do.

Winnie was the sweetest little ferret and everyone who knew her agreed. I miss her so much, and pray this sadness and will ease soon.

Peter
California

 Give fresh food and water at least once a day or even morning and night. Try to gauge how much they will eat each day and don't heap the bowl to the top. That way there won't be wasted food.

WOLF

I awoke this morning to a glorious sunny day. Looking down on the floor next to me, I found Wolf on a black sheet. He was waiting for me to arise. He looked up and nodded his head twice in greeting. Then he stood up next to the bed so I would pick him up and talk to him and hold him. Thus began our day.

We had errands to run today. I placed my intelligent five-pound silver mitt with large brown eyes and black nose in the bathtub with some of his baby blankets and wads of fresh crinkly paper towels. I let the water trickle out. Wolf loves to lap up water trickling from the tub faucet. Then we mock fight amidst the carnage in the bathtub. He places his teeth around my hand and feet around my wrist and we do battle.

After playing amidst the boxes, blankets and toys with all the "monkeys" that are now awake, I clean up poop, food and water bowls, and feed chicken "soup." They all love to sit on my lap and eat this. Then I get ready, whispering to Wolf that just the two of us would go bye-bye. He stood by the carrier I had placed by the front door until I emptied the garbage. Off we went, after cleaning up more poop and more plates.

Everywhere we went, Wolf sat in my lap on his baby blanket. His carrier is next to us in the front seat, should he decide to be there. He lay in my arms or over my shoulder as we went hither and yon. Despite the cancer growing grotesquely under his fur, every person we ran into said, "Is that a ferret? That is the prettiest one I have ever seen." "That's a ferret isn't it? I didn't know they looked like that. That one is really lovely."

He walked on his leash outside in the warm sun. There is no reason to hold onto the leash except for Wolf's safety. He follows me and comes when I call his name. We visited my mother who was delighted to see us. I gave Wolf two big pieces of banana from his grandma.

With so few days remaining of his life, I feel no regrets giving him a treat he has not had for years. He is a big boy, heavy with muscle. His fur is shiny silver, soft and thick. His eyes are bright and expressive. He trots next to me, looking up as I have seen dogs do, to see where I am going. He already has a piece of my heart. I only hope there are bananas in heaven.

Wolf is beginning to choke on his food now. He did not want chicken "soup" for the last three days now. The cancer has taken over; I can easily feel it. I pick him up and kiss him all over. He is so heavy, soft and warm. Every hour now could be his last. I thank God for the gift of this animal. We have lived at the vet's and survived six years I never thought he would see.

It was a beautiful day today—a day spent with my friend.

Lisette
Illinois

NOTE: Wolf died on April 29, 2000, two days after this story was written.

 Ask neighbors and coworkers to save old newspapers for you so you can "paper" the ferret areas, especially the corners of the room. Your friends will probably be thrilled to give you the papers so they don't have to take them to the recycling center.

ZEUS

Zeus passed away in his sleep last night. He was an amazing little guy. He had a very "matter of fact" personality and acted that way. He didn't get too excited over things, but he did like to take you by surprise with his "superman" jump and attack. He was so funny sometimes and quite the lover boy other times. He liked to help with the dishes in the evening. When we would do dishes, Zeus would be put up on the counter and lick up sauces and stuff we'd left behind. He never had too much, but it was good fun for him. He would walk around the appliances, sniff the banana bowl, sometimes attack a potato in the bowl on the counter and generally had a good time. If he wasn't put on the counter quick enough, he would climb the dishwasher, get on the door, grab the top rack and get on the counter. He was definitely a go-getter!

We rescued Zeus and his brother from a bad household. Upon arriving home, Zeus stayed in my arms and was very calm. I think he knew he was home and in a good place. At first, Zeus weighed about two pounds but within a few weeks he had gained one-half pound. He was fluffy and heavy, with smooth beautiful fur.

Zeus' favorite activity was cleaning us, especially the back of a knee or the inside of an elbow. He would do a "closed teeth chew"— lick, lick, lick, and then chomp down and shake his head really hard. We always laughed, and encouraged him to play this game. I loved the shape of his little head and cute little ears.

Even though Zeus had adrenal disease and mast cell tumors, he was always happy to be with us. We gave him treats and he ate like a horse. He was such a cool kid. His Daddy, his brother and I will sorely miss him.

April
Florida

ZEUS

Today Zeus went to The Bridge to join his other family members there. He was a cinnamon sable color about 2 to 3 years old. He loved to be held, gave wonderful kisses, loved to dance, and loved his vitamins and sleep sack.

Zeus had surgery today for adrenal disease and came through the surgery just fine. Two hours later, however, he had a seizure that took his life.

Zeus, look for the others that are already across The Bridge. They will gather you to them and the party will begin. Rest in peace my Zeus, we love you.

Sandi
Florida

 Check dishwashers, clothes dryers, front loading washers and refrigerators before closing the doors or using them. Ferrets love to climb inside appliances and can easily get trapped inside if you are not careful. Before running the dishwasher, check both the upper and lower racks and pull out the bottom rack to check underneath for fuzzy feet before closing the door.

ZIGGY

I have tried several times to write this story since my fiancé and I helped our dear sweet Ziggy to The Bridge last Saturday.

Ziggy was diagnosed with heart disease, insulinoma and adrenal disease in October 2001. A few weeks ago, we decided against adrenal surgery and to keep Zig as comfortable as possible. A week ago, I found him lying in his own excrement in the midst of an insulinomic seizure. When he came out of it, he lacked the strength to make it to the corner. We stayed up with him throughout the night. In the morning, we knew it was time.

I held him during the hour and a half drive to the vet's office. He seemed content in my arms, as I told him about the Rainbow Bridge and all the good things that awaited him. At times, he pushed his nose against my neck, hiding his head under my chin. As we pulled into the vet's parking lot, he whimpered once, and then returned to his calm state. The vet's office usually elicited some response from him, but not this time. It was the most relaxed we had ever seen him. As he slipped away from us, I held his little head and paws and told him how great he was and how much we'd miss him.

It will be a week tomorrow since he left this world, and my heart aches more than I ever imagined it could. Ziggy was our first ferret and my best friend. It takes great effort to remind myself that he is in a better place, where he can have all the cranberry raisins his little heart desires and has enough energy to zip through tubes all afternoon. I worry that he is lonely there, because he was a Momma's boy and always clung to me when he was somewhere new. He was never very fond of other fuzzbuns.

God, please tell Ziggy that we love him and that we did the best we could for him. I will miss our naps together, belly tickles and playing "foot monster." Daddy misses his "moose." Goodbye, my sweet baby. You will be forever in my heart.

Crystal
Massachusetts

ZIGGY

My old man, Ziggy the ferret, passed away early this morning on Thursday, May 9, 2002. He was deaf, blind, and couldn't smell much, but he certainly didn't let that stop him. He loved to chase the cat, roam around the house, and see what new place he could find to sneak into. He was a very friendly ferret, willing to play with anyone and never starting a fight. Another star now lights up the night sky.

I know he's gone, but I still keep expecting him to make his rounds, looking for snacks to stash in his sleep sack. Just a small dab of vitamins would take him a one-half hour to finish, because he just liked the idea that he was getting attention. His cagemates keep looking for him to curl up with (he was one warm ferret to sleep with), and the food bowl doesn't look quite so empty each morning.

Ziggy was a very sweet ferret. His big head and silly antics will provide many memories for me. I hope the sorrow that his buddies feel will fade with time, and that they won't miss him quite so much. He died in his sleep, so I'm sure that he was having one of his happy dreams that he seemed to have all of the time.

God, please watch over Ziggy at the Rainbow Bridge. Stand by him when he sees all the wonderful bright colors, smells the fantastic smells and hears all those sounds of fun and happiness for the first time in his life. Then, stand back as he grabs the nearest basketball and does a hangin' dunk. You go, Ziggy boy!

Todd
Pennsylvania

Wash all bedding frequently. Ferrets love clean hammocks, blankets and sweatshirts. This will also help alleviate ear mites. Use laundry detergent with no perfume scent. Highly scented detergent could be harmful to your ferret's sensitive respiratory system.

ZORRO

I've always known this would happen, but knowing can never prepare you for the inevitable. I lost my first ferret today.

When I went to feed the fuzzies this morning, Zorro was curled up in one corner of the cage and didn't get up with the others when they came to the door to greet me. When I called his name, he still wouldn't move. My baby was so fond of pulling the "dead ferret" trick on me. I thought he was just having some fun with his Mommy, but he wasn't. At least I have the comfort of feeling sure he didn't go painfully. It looked like he just lay down to sleep and didn't wake up.

He was the sweetest little sable boy you'd ever want to meet. He was always smaller than the other boys, but that didn't make him any less tough or energetic. I remember when we first got him seven years ago—he was such a darling little ball of fluff and was Mommy's boy. I was doing my undergraduate work at the time, and I would lie on my bed to study. When Zorro would tire from playing, he would crawl into my shirt and lie next to my tummy for a nap. He continued this habit over the years. I'm going to miss having that little warm fuzzy body under my shirt and next to my tummy.

God, please keep an eye out for Zorro. He doesn't have any brothers or sisters up there to greet him, so he might be lonely at first. He was always the first to greet a newbie, so I'm sure he'll make new friends quickly. Could you be sure he finds some granola bars, since he never did care much for raisins? And God, tell him his mommy loves him very much and will always miss him. Thanks.

Lisa Mom
Georgia

ZUZU

In 1991, we purchased our first ferret—an albino with the sweetest personality. Her name was ZuZu. My son, who was 3 years old at the time, could not be separated from this tiny creature. For several years she became a regular at school for "show and tell."

At age 4, ZuZu had surgery to remove a benign growth from her neck, and she recovered nicely. Her constant playful ways made us love her more and more as the years passed. Approximately one year ago, she began to lose her hair as a result of adrenal disease and became totally bald. She was a frightful sight, but she never stopped giving everyone greetings and kisses. Because ZuZu was now nearly 10 years old, she would not likely survive surgery. We gave her the best treatment and lots of love; we knew she would soon be gone.

As ZuZu snuggled in her in her favorite blanket, she grew more tired each day. She became so weak, I started to feed her with an eyedropper and gave her Pedialyte to keep her hydrated. On Christmas Eve, she became very ill and drifted in and out of sleep. As was our family tradition, I lit Christmas candles to invite Christmas into our home. I also lit one for ZuZu and said a little prayer, so her suffering would end and the Lord would take her peacefully. To my surprise, at 12:03 A.M. on Christmas morning, her candle burned out. When I checked on her in her bed, I noticed she had passed away. We will love her forever and she will always be our little Christmas angel.

We now have two new baby ferrets. I think one of them is ZuZu all over again, and we are once again ready for years of love with the new members of our family.

The Hamilton Family
New Jersey

Fuzzbean Crossing

Ferret on a Cloud

THE DANCE

Looking back on the memory of
The dance we shared 'neath the stars above
For a moment all the world was right
How could I have known that you'd ever say goodbye

And now I'm glad I didn't know
The way it all would end the way it all would go
Our lives are better left to chance
I could have missed the pain
But I'd of had to miss the dance

                                            - Tony Arata

APPENDIX

DEALING WITH GRIEF

Any loss is a difficult one, whether it is the loss of a job, separation of friends, death of a family member or cherished pet. Generally, we cope better with a loss we have anticipated. A sudden, unexpected loss is much more difficult. There are several stages we must go through when experiencing loss—denial, anger, bargaining, guilt, depression, and acceptance.

When dealing with the loss of a pet, it is the pets that interact most with the family that seem to elicit the most emotional upheaval. When a pet goldfish, turtle, or gerbil dies, it is not nearly as difficult a loss as that of a dog, cat, ferret or other companion animal. These animals become so much a part of our day-to-day living; we find our life is changed drastically when they are no longer around. Adjusting to a new daily routine after a loss is a difficult task. There will be little reminders of our pet's existence everywhere. It might be a favorite toy that now lies on the carpet unused, the pet food in the cupboard that you put in the bowl each day, or maybe you lost your best snuggle buddy at bedtime. After all, pets offer us unconditional love and companionship and we tend to form strong emotional bonds with them.

It is impossible for some people to understand that the loss of a pet is as difficult as that a loss of a family member but, for many of us, the loss is as difficult, if not more so. It doesn't mean we loved our family member less or our pet more, it means we had a strong emotional attachment to both of them. Family members, friends, and co-workers may not be as supportive and sympathetic as you would like them to be when you experience a loss of a pet. Unfortunately, an animal's life is not regarded as being equal to a human's life to many people. All life is precious, and should be regarded as such, no matter what species it may be.

Whether the pet has been with you a short while or for many years, everyone in the family will surely be affected by the loss. The intense emotional feelings that accompany a loss are a normal part of the grieving period. Some people are able to cope with loss easier than others, and will move on with their daily routine rather quickly. Others may find that the feelings of sadness are always at hand, and certain experiences will trigger an emotional outbreak. Everyone expresses loss differently and it cannot be predicted how anyone will feel after the loss of a pet. Some people are detached, which is one way of coping with the loss.

When a person dies, we have rituals like viewings, wakes, and funerals. When a pet dies, there are no such formalities. You may find it therapeutic to hold a private ceremony at home for your pet. It might be as simple as a backyard burial or a candlelight ceremony with family members or a few friends. It could also be more elaborate, like a burial in a public pet cemetery. Whatever you do, it will have meaning to you at the time and, it will add immeasurable value to the memories you have of your pet.

Many times, getting another pet immediately lessens the profound sadness and pain. Occasionally, individuals find they cannot replace the pet that died, and may never get another one. If they do eventually get another pet, it may not happen for a long time. Since each pet is unique, a new family pet can never replace the one that is no longer with us. But, rather, it occupies our time and our mind so we don't dwell on our sorrow as much.

Whether you have lost one pet or many, the grief does not lessen with each one. Grief does not magically disappear, but must be given time to heal. It is part of the grieving process to first deny the reality of death and then become angry, either internally or at others. Bargaining with God may be part of your grieving. Having feelings of guilt, thinking you could have done more to intervene and help your pet are normal. It is customary to feel depressed and, in some cases, it may be necessary to seek professional help if the depression continues. During this time of grief:

- ♥ Give yourself permission to grieve
- ♥ Memorialize your pet
- ♥ Get plenty of rest
- ♥ Eat nutritious food
- ♥ Talk to people who understand your loss (search "pet loss" on the Internet to find many compassion sites, talk to your veterinarian or local humane society to find bereavement counseling in your area)

- Indulge yourself in small pleasures
- Be patient with yourself—grief has no time limit
- Don't be afraid to ask for help

Finally, you will go through the recovery stage and will accept the loss. This is when you will have fond memories of the happy times you and your pet shared. It will become easier to look at the precious photographs you have of your pet and think about how much they meant to you. You will now be able to form new emotional ties with a new pet.

When someone talks to you about their loss of a pet, stop what you are doing and pay attention to their needs. Talk quietly and do not rush off to get back to your activity. Instead, listen to them, give comfort, and be sensitive to their grief. Treat them as you wish to be treated in the same situation. Send a handwritten note of condolence; it is very special when someone has experienced a loss.

Grief is confusing, frustrating and emotional. You are not alone in your feelings of grief, and what you feel is entirely normal. You will get through it!

BOOKS ON GRIEF

Goodbye, Dear Friend, Coming to Terms with the Death of a Pet, Virginia Ironside, Robson Books Ltd., 1994

> This thoughtful book covers every aspect of the loss of a pet including euthanasia, burial, and cremation. It also includes beautiful poetry.

Goodbye, Friend: Healing Wisdom for Anyone Who Has Lost a Pet, Gary Kowalski

> Compassionate advice to get you through the loss of your pet can be found in this book. There are ideas for rituals and ceremonies, spiritual guidance, plus readings and poetry also included.

Healing Grief, James Van Praagh, Button, New York, NY, April 2000

> A wonderful book dealing with loss, grief and healing, written by James Van Praagh, a renowned medium. There are several pages of great pet stories in this book. He writes about euthanasia and gives guidelines for healing oneself after the loss of a pet.

It's Okay to Cry, Maria L. King, Maria L. Quintana, Shari L. Veleba, Harley G. King

> Read the warm stories that help people find hope and healing when dealing with the death of a pet. Sixty-two stories are included in this book, written by people who have lost dogs, cats, horses, birds, and other animals.

Legacies of Love, A Gentle Guide to Healing from the Loss of Your Animal, Teresa L. Wagner and Maxine Musgrave

> This book portrays a compelling message of hope and renewal during the difficult time of loss. You will find understanding and support for those who have lost pets on these pages.

The Resting Place: Pet Cemeteries and Memorials, Michele Lanci-Altomare, Bowtie Press

> Award-winning photographer, Lanci-Altomare shows images of pet memorials around the country and in England. Excerpts from people who have lost pets, stories from pet cemetery owners and poetry abound here. This book is beautiful, intriguing, and inspirational.

The Soul of Your Pet, Scott S. Smith, December 1998

> Evidence of the survival of animals after death is the subject of this book.

COMMON MEDICAL CONDITIONS IN FERRETS

Listed below are the most common medical conditions found in ferrets. This is not a complete listing of every possible medical condition and your ferret may experience other conditions than those listed here.

Medical Condition	Description	Signs to Look For
Adrenal Disease/ Tumor	Usually it is the left adrenal gland that is affected. Although not uncommon, the right adrenal gland can also be diseased. Ferrets can live after having one or both adrenal glands removed.	♥ Hair loss on the tail, top of the tailbone or across the shoulders ♥ Your ferret feels warmer to the touch than normal ♥ Swollen vulva ♥ Straining to urinate ♥ Itchy skin ♥ Aggressive behavior *Note:* Any hair loss on the body can be a possible sign of an adrenal tumor, but it could simply be a seasonal hair loss.

Medical Condition	Description	Signs to Look For
Aleutian's Disease (ADV)	ADV is a parvo virus and is spread through saliva, feces, urine and the placenta. Take precautions to avoid exposing your ferret to ADV. Do not let your ferret play with ferrets that have not tested negative for ADV. Do not let strangers handle your ferret and do not handle their ferrets. Keep your ferret in a carrier while at the vet, except in the exam room. Have your ferrets tested for Aleutian's Disease through a saliva or blood test. Currently there is no treatment, vaccine or cure for ADV.	♥ Chronic progressive wasting ♥ Hind end paralysis ♥ Muscle wasting ♥ Tremors ♥ Urinary incontinence ♥ Lethargy ♥ Enlarged spleen ♥ Black tarry feces ♥ Sometimes there will be no visible signs
Anemia	Anemia is caused by a low blood count and can cause your ferret to be tired and sleep a lot. A simple blood test can detect anemia and supplements can be given to alleviate this condition.	♥ Lethargy ♥ Sleeping more than usual ♥ White or very pale pink nose, ears and foot pads

Medical Condition	Description	Signs to Look For
Dental Conditions	Ferret teeth collect tartar, especially on the back teeth. Tartar can be removed by your veterinarian while the ferret is sedated. Older ferrets will have more tartar and dirtier teeth. Swelling of the face could mean an infection is present in the mouth. Antibiotics or surgery may be necessary.	♥ Difficulty chewing ♥ Eating less than usual ♥ Weight loss ♥ Swelling anywhere on the face or around the head
Epizootic Catarrhal Enteritis (ECE) Also known as the *green diarrhea virus*	ECE is a viral infection and is usually noticed when a new ferret comes into the household. The new ferret or ones already living there may exhibit symptoms. Older ferrets will experience the severest problems and youngest ferrets the mildest. Dehydration comes very quickly and it is important to get your ferret to your vet quickly to start them on fluids, antibiotics and a bland diet.	♥ Green and watery stools ♥ Weight loss ♥ Loss of appetite ♥ Lethargy ♥ Vomiting

Medical Condition	Description	Signs to Look For
Enlarged Lymph Nodes	Infection, inflammation or cancer can caused enlarged lymph nodes. Sometimes you can feel the enlarged lymph nodes under your ferret's jaw or other external locations. This condition can also be detected through x-rays and exploratory surgery.	♥ Weight loss ♥ Lethargy ♥ Loose stools ♥ Lumps under the jaws, armpits or behind the knees
Hairball or Foreign Body	Since ferrets groom themselves regularly, they can get hairballs. Occasionally, like cats, ferrets will throw up a hairball, but this is uncommon. Give your ferret cat hairball remedy regularly. Foreign bodies are caused by your ferret eating something it shouldn't. Do not let them play with rubber or latex toys. Don't leave rubber bands lying around within your ferret's reach. Obstructions generally require surgery. This condition is life threatening if not treated quickly.	♥ Decreased appetite ♥ Loose stools ♥ Weight loss ♥ Vomiting ♥ Tucked and painful abdomen

Medical Condition	Description	Signs to Look For
Insulinoma	Tumors on the pancreas which release insulin and cause low blood sugar. Your ferret can be tested for low blood sugar with a simple blood test. Insulinoma tumors must be surgically removed.	♥ Sleeping more than usual ♥ Low energy level ♥ Wobbly when walking ♥ Dragging the hind legs ♥ Falling over ♥ Unable to stand ♥ Seizure ♥ Coma
Intestinal or Liver Abnormalities	These can be found by getting your ferret a Complete Blood Count (CBC) panel, x-rays, ultrasound or through exploratory surgery. Portions of the liver can be removed and your ferret can still lead a fairly normal life.	♥ Loose stools ♥ Weight loss ♥ Poor appetite

Medical Condition	Description	Signs to Look For
Prolapsed Rectum	This is caused by straining while defecating, fighting with another ferret or from a poor diet. For a temporary solution, it can be corrected with sutures, but generally this is not permanent. Try putting about a teaspoon of sugar in a basin of about 2 cups of comfortably warm water and soak your ferret's bottom in it for as long as they will sit still. Rinse the sticky bottom with some warm water. Repeat in one-half hour or as necessary. This should alleviate the condition. If this doesn't work, get some Myrrh or White Oak Bark tincture at the health food store and put a dropperful in some warm water. Soak your ferret's bottom in the mixture for a few minutes.	♥ Your ferret's rectum appears swollen or is protruding outside the body ♥ Dragging or rubbing their rear end on the carpet (dragging the rear end is normal after they've just used the litter box) ♥ Persistent straining to defecate

Medical Condition	Description	Signs to Look For
Spleen Tumors	A common condition which can be corrected by surgically removing the spleen. This is called a splenectomy. Spleen tumors can cause the abdomen to become enlarged. *Note*: Ferrets can have large spleens without having a spleen tumor.	♥ Your ferret has a "pear shape" ♥ Ribs and backsides appear distended ♥ Stomach and underbelly area are larger than normal *Note*: Use caution when handling your ferret, do not palpitate or grab your ferret by the abdomen. This could cause rupturing of the spleen.

The above conditions are serious and require medical attention. Sometimes your ferret can have more than one condition simultaneously. Consult an experienced ferret-friendly veterinarian to learn your options and to decide the best treatment for your ferret.

MEDICATIONS USED FOR TREATING FERRETS

The medications listed below are used for treating a variety of medical conditions in ferrets. A brief explanation is given for each medication.

Never give your ferrets medications without first consulting your veterinarian. Check expiration dates of medications in the cupboard and refrigerator periodically and throw away those medications that have expired.

Medication	Usage
Amoxicillin	A liquid antibiotic used for infections and after-surgery recovery
Brewers Yeast	Source of chromium to stabilize glucose and insulin for ferrets with insulinoma
Carafate	A liquid used to protect damaged cells; used for ulcers or other stomach problems
Clavamox	A liquid antibiotic used for infections and after-surgery recovery
Cortisone	Steroid medication used as an anti-inflammatory to treat cancer
Flagyl	An antibiotic used to treat diarrhea and ulcers
Lupron	A long-acting injection used to treat adrenal tumors

Medication	Usage
Orbax	A liquid antibiotic used for infections and after-surgery recovery
Pediapred	An liquid steroid medication used as a hormone replace supplement
Percorten	Hormone replacement injection given every 3-4 weeks for ferrets that have had both adrenal glands removed. Without this injection, your ferret may exhibit poor appetite, weight loss and lethargy and their condition can quickly become life-threatening.
Pet-Tinic	Iron supplement used to treat anemia
Prednisone	An liquid steroid medication used as an anti-inflammatory to treat cancer
Proglycem	An liquid medication used to treat insulinoma

THE ACUPUNCTURE TREATMENT AS TOLD BY JAKOB

Hi, my name is Jakob. I am an albino ferret who was adopted by my Mom in January 1998, when I was just a baby. Before I found my current Mom, I was lost and alone, wandering the streets of Baltimore, MD. Luckily, there wasn't any snow at that time because no one would have been able to see me since I'm so snowy white. I was having a very hard time hobbling around; only my two back legs and one of my front legs worked. My other front leg had been fractured in a previous accident and had atrophied in a curled-up position under my body and hung quite limp. I had no use of this leg and was unable to put any weight on it. I was filthy dirty, shivering from the cold and trying to find my way back home to my family and my own warm bed.

You can imagine how excited and happy I was when someone found me, picked me up off the streets and took me to the ferret shelter. I looked like I was wearing black socks because my feet and legs were so dirty and my eyes and ears were ringed with soot. I was given a bath at the shelter which I didn't like much. It was tough living on the streets, even for a short while. It sure felt good afterward, when I was nice and clean and had lots of food to eat. My tummy began to feel so much better. I had a nice cozy hammock to sleep in and there were other ferrets just like me. The nice lady at the ferret shelter soon found me a new "forever" Mom.

My new Mom didn't know how I was going to get along in my new house because my room was upstairs. She knew I would have trouble getting up the stairs by myself because of my useless leg.

The next day, just when I started getting situated in my new home, I was put in a carrier along with two of my new brothers and sisters. I hoped I wasn't going to be sent away again or, worse yet, left out in the cold again. We went to visit a lady who was an acupuncturist and Mommy said I was a very brave boy. I received something called a "treatment" which she hoped would help my injured and useless leg. I didn't feel anything and the lady was very nice to me.

When I got back home after my acupuncture treatment I tried putting my front leg down on the floor to see if I could step on it. It felt very strange because my leg was very stiff from not walking on it for so long. Within two days I realized I could walk gently on the leg again and it got better and easier each time I tried to step down on my foot. Soon, I was able to use my leg fully again. I even began jumping over the "wall" to get out of my room when I woke up from my nap. None of the other furry kids had ever been able to scale the wall before I did. Mom said she was amazed at how strong my leg had become and she called me her "miracle boy."

Today I'm a healthy big boy about 5 years old and am active and happy. Even now, I can still jump the two-foot barricade at the entrance to my room as gracefully as ever. I showed a couple of my buddies how to scale the wall, but I'm not showing the rest of the bunch here. It's going to be my little secret.

Love,
Jakob

TOXIC PLANTS

The common house plants listed below are toxic to pets. Check your home, especially around the holidays, to make sure none of these plants is within reach of your ferrets or other pets in the household.

Aloe Vera
Apple Seeds
Apricot pits
Avocado
Azalea
Baby's Breath
Caladium
Calla Lily
Cherry (pits, seeds and wilting leaves)
Christmas Rose
Chrysanthemum
Clematis
Delphinium
Dieffenbachia
Easter Lily
Eggplant
English Ivy
Eucalyptus
Evergreen
Ferns
Geranium
Holly
Hyacinth
Hydrangea
Iris
Marigold
Mistletoe
Peach (pits and wilting leaves)
Philodendron
Poinsettia
Rubber Plant
Schefflera
Sweetpea
Tobacco
Tomato Plant (green fruit, stem and leaves)
Tulip
Wisteria

HELPFUL CHARTS

NAIL CLIPPING AND EAR CLEANING CHART

This is a useful chart if you need to keep track of several ferrets in the household. Keep this chart handy on the refrigerator so you can keep up to date on nail clipping and ear cleaning. Clip nails one week and ears the next. This way you don't have to be overwhelmed with the maintenance all at one time. It's helpful to have a regular day to do this each week, like Saturday or Sunday. Once you get in the habit of doing this weekly maintenance, it will be done quickly and you can spend the rest of the day enjoying and playing with your ferrets. As you do each task, put a checkmark in the box under the ferret's name.

	Maxx	Ozzie	Pogo	Riki	Rory	Sami
Nails	✓	✓	✓	✓	✓	✓
Ears	✓		✓	✓		✓
Nails						
Ears						
Nails						
Ears						
Nails						
Ears						

Add extra columns to your chart for additional ferrets. Hang your chart on the refrigerator with magnetic strips so it is within easy reach when you need it each week.

WEIGHT CHART

The weight chart below is easy to create by hand or on the computer. It is invaluable when keeping track of each ferret's weight each month. Just watch to make sure that no one is losing or gaining more than an ounce or two from month to month. If there is a significant weight loss during one month or over a couple of months, consult your veterinarian. You don't want a fat ferret, because added weight is unhealthy for them. It is normal for young ferrets to gain several ounces in a single month or during a few months time, while they are still growing and their body is filling out. Free-roaming ferrets may be thinner than caged ferrets, due to the increased amount of exercise they get.

	Angel (5 yrs.)	Annie (4 yrs.)	Danny (3 yrs.)	Edd (1 yr.)	Hershey (3 yrs.)
Jan.	1 lb. 10 oz.	2 lb. 1 oz.	2 lb. 10 oz.	2 lb. 12 oz.	2 lb. 8 oz.
Feb.	1 lb. 6 oz.	2 lb. 3 oz.	2 lb. 11 oz.	2 lb. 10 oz.	2 lb. 8 oz.
Mar.					
Apr.					
May					
June					
July					
Aug					
Sept.					
Oct.					
Nov.					
Dec.					

Notice how each ferret's age is also written under their name at the top of the weight chart. This makes it easier to keep track of ages when you have several ferrets. Many times, you will not know the age, especially if you have rescue ferrets. Just estimate on January 1 each year, when you make a new chart, each ferret's age if you are unsure.

Angel's weight loss shown on the previous page would be significant, especially combined with her current age of 4 years.

MEDICATION CHART

Make a chart to keep track of your ferret's medication, whether you have one or many ferrets. You will need one chart for each day during the period you are administering the medications. Most meds are given for a two-week period or longer. Some medications are given for an indefinite period of time. To make a month of charts using a computer, do the following:

- ♥ Create one chart with the information you need for each ferret
- ♥ Copy your chart and paste enough times to make another chart for the remaining days of the month
- ♥ If you still need to give medications the following month, make another batch of charts for the next month

Type the "Xs" on the chart when you are making it, not when the ferrets get their medication. Make as many "Xs" as you have doses of medication to give. Notice on September 1, Jakob gets one dose of Pediapred, two doses of Pet-Tinic and two doses of amoxicillin; Jayme gets Pet-Tinic once a day and Tabbi gets Pediapred once a day. Once you have the "Xs" on the chart, just scratch out each "X" as you give the meds.

At the top of the first chart on the page, indicate the dosage of each medication. If you are using a computer, create a header with the dosage information. This will enable you to type the information once but repeat it automatically on the remaining pages. Make note of any differences in the amount of medication each ferret gets directly in the box beneath their name and next to the "X." In the example below, Jakob gets only .5cc of Pet-Tinic twice a day while Jayme gets 1cc once a day.

These charts make it easy to keep track of who gets what medication and how many times to administer it each day.

| Pediapred = .3cc | Pet-Tinic = 1cc | Amoxicillin = .5cc |

Sun., 9/1	Pediapred	Pet-Tinic®	Amoxicillin
Jakob	X	X X (.5cc)	X X
Jayme		X	
Tabbi	X		

Mon., 9/2	Pediapred	Pet-Tinic®	Amoxicillin
Jakob	X	X X (.5cc)	X X
Jayme		X	
Tabbi	X		

Tues., 9/3	Pediapred	Pet-Tinic®	Amoxicillin
Jakob	X	X X (.5cc)	X X
Jayme		X	
Tabbi	X		

If you need to give additional medications, add more columns. If additional ferrets need medication, add more rows.

INSTRUCTIONS & PATTERNS

CREATING A FERRET ROOM

If you have an extra bedroom in the house, it would make a perfect room to house the ferrets. They need a place of their own instead of your bedroom with wall-to-wall newspapers for pooping. Because ferrets are social animals like dogs and cats, they prefer to be around family members as much as possible. If you don't have to keep them in a cage due to space limitations or other considerations, creating a ferret room makes their life so much better. The ferret room can serve as a place for them to sleep and be a secure area for them when you are at work or away from home.

The room does not need to be large because when ferrets are in their room, they will sleep most of the time, just like when they are confined in a cage.

The first thing to do is remove all doors from the room. Removing the door hardware is optional but it does make the room look better with it removed. Next, look at the floor. Do you have wall-to-wall carpeting or some other type of flooring that will be destroyed if it gets wet? If you have carpet in the room, remove it and replace it with a seamless vinyl floor. Carpet holds the dirt and will become damaged beyond repair or cleaning with constant urination from your furry whiskered ones. If you have carpet in the room, very quickly it could become hazardous to the ferrets living there, as well as your own health. If you install a vinyl floor, use vinyl cove base molding all around the room to finish it off instead of wood molding. Cove base molding can be found at home improvement centers or carpet stores. This helps you keep the room cleaner because ferret poop gets in the strangest places, even up the wall at times. I still don't know how they do that. You may also want to freshen up the room with a coat of paint. Use semi-gloss or satin because it is easier to clean.

Keep furniture to a minimum in the room. A small table for supplies would be useful, but even better would be shelves attached to the wall. On the shelf, put trash bags, throw rugs for the floor and extra bedding. Furniture in the room will eliminate some of space the ferrets have to play in. Don't have anything in the room that your ferrets could climb on and possibly fall and injure themselves.

Put shades, blinds or draperies on any windows to darken the room for good ferret naps. Don't keep them in constant darkness; all creatures need sunlight and daylight to thrive. If you decide to put curtains or draperies on the windows, make sure they are short enough to keep them out of the ferret's reach.

If there is a closet in the room, turn this into the sleeping "den." Purchase a small tension rod and hang a curtain on the closet door because ferrets like to sleep where it is dark. Use blankets or a comforter for bedding in the closet. If you use a comforter, make sure all seams are intact without holes or worn spots in the fabric that can easily be torn by ferret nails. You would not want your ferret to get inside a comforter and be unable to find their way out.

Ferrets enjoy the security of a pet carrier filled with soft bedding, like old sweatshirts, for sleeping. They also like to "bed hop" and move from bed to bed during naptime to find the most comfortable spot, or to cuddle up with the most comfortable ferret.

Cages can be put in the room to hang hammocks for cozy sleeping. Secure the door of a cage open using a tiny bungee cord which can be easily removed if necessary. Food and water bowls can be placed in cages, in a central location in the room or both. It is preferable to have food and water in a cage as well as on the ferret room floor, to enable the ferrets sleeping in the cages to get a quick drink or nibble of kibble.

The final step in setting up your ferret room is to put a barricade at the door into the room so you can keep them confined whenever necessary. Since you have already removed the door, nail a 40-48" length of quarter round (available from the home improvement center or hardware store) to the doorjamb on the inside of the room. One end of the quarter round should begin at the floor and the other end will be part way up the doorjamb. Leave a little more than ½" of space from the center portion of the doorjamb to create a channel to slide the barricade up and down. For the barricade, cut a piece of ½" thick plywood to the width of your door minus a small clearance for smooth sliding. Usually this will be about 30" wide, the width of a standard door. The height will depend upon your personal preference. Make the height as high as you can step over comfortably but the ferrets cannot climb over.

If the barricade is at least two feet high, most of the ferrets will not be able to hoist themselves over it. Cut two pieces of ½" thick plywood exactly the same size. This way, you can put a double barricade up, one stacked on top of the other for nighttime security and for safety when you are at work. One barricade piece has a 4" high x 6" wide hole cut along the edge of the widest side (along the floor side) and centered (see drawing below). This enables the ferrets to go freely in and out of their room, but keeps out the cats so they don't eat the ferret food. If you have other pets in the household, this is a good solution. You can easily step over the barricade to go in and out of the room for cleaning or for counting noses before going off to work. Before leaving home, make sure the double barricade is always in place. Take care when using the barricade to make sure there are no fuzzy ones standing in the doorway to get their toes pinched.

Instead of having two pieces of plywood as suggested, you may prefer to cut one piece a little higher than two feet, but short enough so you can still step over it. Cut a 4" x 6" hole in one long edge to keep other family pets out but let ferrets in and out. When you want to secure the ferrets in their room, just lift the barricade up and reverse it so the small "ferret doorway" is at the top instead of the floor edge (see drawing below). Observe your ferrets to make sure that the ferret opening at the top is not so low that your ferrets can jump over the barricade.

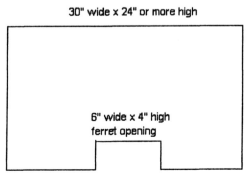

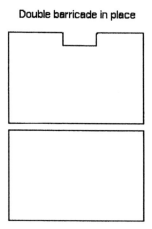

Double barricade in place

Paint the barricade and quarter round a complementary color to the room so it is a nice addition to your home. If you are artistic, draw or paint flowers, a scene or something ferrety on the hallway side of the barricade for a decorative effect.

Depending on how many ferrets will be housed in the room, have one, two or more small portable cages in the room at all times with hammocks and bedding. These will be used for sleeping most of the time, but could also serve as a container for ferrets if you had an emergency such as a fire, and had to get them out of the house quickly. The best place for the ferret room is on the first floor, if possible. It would be easier to break a window, if necessary, to get them outdoors to safety.

A pillowcase could also serve as a quick way to get a few ferrets out of the house quickly in an emergency. Put a pillowcase or two on a closet shelf or somewhere else in the room where it is easily accessible to you and not the ferrets. In case of emergency, grab the pillowcase, grab the ferrets and go to a safe place.

Lastly, put litter boxes in all the corners of the room, including any large cages. Secure the litter boxes in the cages with bungee cords so they won't be tipped over by your talented and strong ferrets. Put washable throw rugs on the floor for comfortable walking, a non-tipping freshly-filled water dish and plenty of their favorite ferret food within easy reach. You may also want to line the edges of the room with newspaper for easy cleanup of accidents. If you have a difficult time gathering enough news-papers for lining ferret or other rooms, ask neighbors or co-workers to save them for you. They'll be happy to accommodate you so they won't have to make another trip to the recycling center.

Congratulations, you have just completed a very easy-to-clean, comfortable and safe environment for your ferrets.

NOTE: Soon you will find that the ferret room becomes the cleanest room the house. If you have so many ferrets that you have a dedicated ferret room, you will find yourself too busy to clean the rest of the house and too exhausted to care if it's not spotless.

HOW TO MAKE FLEECE "DOUBLE STUFF" FERRET HAMMOCKS

Soft and cozy washable fleece fabric comes in great colors and cute patterns, and can be purchased at any fabric store and at many discount department stores. An advantage to using fleece over other materials is that the fabric does not ravel or fall apart when cut or laundered. From one yard of fleece you can make four "double stuff" sleeping bag hammocks or eight single-layer hammocks. Your cost will be from 90 cents each (single layer) to $2.00 or less each (double hammocks) from only a yard of fabric. One yard of fleece costs approximately $7 to $12 depending upon fabric weight and pattern. Frequently you can find it on sale at the fabric store. It helps to have a sewing machine because the stitching is faster, but it is not necessary. To make the hammocks, follow the steps below. The instructions below are for making "double stuff" sleeping bag hammocks. Your fuzzy kids can climb inside the hammock or lie on top of it.

1. Cut a piece of fleece fabric approximately 18" x 27".[39]

2. Fold it in half on the short side. You will now have a rectangle approximately 18" x 14".

3. Stitch together both short sides using a 1/2" seam.

4. Fold over the opening once about 1/2" all the way around and stitch to make a hem (this should look something like a small pillowcase now with an opening at the widest end).

---

[39] For a custom measurement to your exact specifications, measure the cage where the hammock will hang .

5. Turn the hammock right side out and stitch a small buttonhole at each corner. With a razorblade or sharp craft knife, make a slit between the stitching to open the buttonhole. You can also insert metal grommets at each of the hammock's four corners, if desired, instead of making buttonholes.

6. Use metal shower curtain hooks which are available from home improvement centers or bed and bath stores to suspend your cozy ferret hammock from a cage.

7. Watch the ferrets happily climb inside and quickly begin dreaming about ferret treats.

For making single-layer fleece fabric hammocks, cut a piece of sturdy fabric to fit comfortably inside your cage. Next, fold over all edges and stitch to create a hem (see note below). Make a buttonhole on each corner or insert grommets. Now you're ready to hang and use the hammock. Goodnight and sweet dreams.

NOTE: When using a single layer of fabric for your hammock, it is advisable to make the hems large enough so you will have a double layer where the grommets or buttonholes will go. This way there is less chance of the grommets tearing the fabric with usage and laundering.

HOW TO MAKE COZY FERRET SLEEPING BAGS

Children's sweatpants make perfect sleeping bags for your ferrets because they are soft, warm, and easily washable. Look for sweatpants on sale at discount department stores for $2 to $4. Size three is just the right size to hold up to two of your sleepy furry kids. These sweatpants are such a bargain and so cozy, plus the ferrets don't care what color you buy. In just a few minutes, you will be able to make the sleeping bag and watch your fuzzies snuggle up inside and stay toasty warm. All you need is a pair of scissors and a sewing machine or a needle and thread.

Read the instructions below and look on the next page for the cutting and stitching diagram.

1. Get a pair of children's sweatpants, approximately size three, and turn them inside out, laying them flat on a table.

2. Cut off the elasticized ankle cuffs close to the seams.

3. Cut off the stitching at the inside of the legs, clipping close to the seam.

NOTE: The elastic waist will remain uncut and be used for the opening of the sleeping bag.

4. Grab the pants at the center on both sides, spread apart and flatten on the table once again. Stitch around all raw cut edges.

   NOTE: You may need to trim the fabric slightly before sewing, so there is a smooth transition from the top to the bottom of the bag where the stitching will be done. Look at diagram 4 on the next page to see the finished shape.

   5. Turn right side out and now you have a warm and inexpensive sleeping bag for your little fuzzbunnies.

Fuzzbean Crossing

1

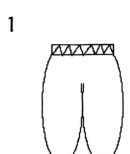

2

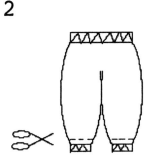

3

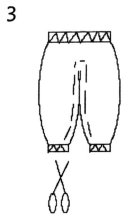

4

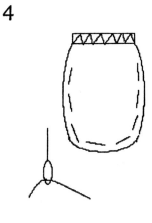

WONDERFUL WEBSITES TO VISIT

Grief

1. www.animalsinourhearts.com

    This is a pet loss and animal communication resource site. In addition to celebrating the joy and wonder of the animal/human relationship, you will also find a pet loss audiobook on this website.

2. www.findinfo.com/petloss.htm

    Articles about pet loss, memoriam links, organizations, poetry, stories, hotlines, counselors, and other pet loss topics will be found here.

3. www.griefhealing.com

    This site contains an extensive listing of general pet loss resources, help lines, message boards and chats.

4. www.petloss.com

    This is a gentle and compassionate website for pet lovers who are grieving over the loss of a pet. Here you will find the pet loss candle ceremony, message board, healing and inspirational poetry, and more.

Medical Information and Facilities

1. www.afip.org/ferrets

    Check this site for simple directions on feeding sick ferrets. You will also find good information on some ferret diseases for caretakers and veterinarians alike.

2. www.bradleyhills.com or www.ferretdoctor.com

This is the website of Charles A. Weiss, DVM, world-renowned ferret specialist at Bradley Hills Animal Hospital, 7210 Bradley Boulevard, Bethesda, MD, 301-365-5448. This site contains medical information and an instructional video for vets on common ferret surgical procedures such as insulinoma and adrenal disease.

Memorial Gardens

1. www.creatures.com/cemetery.html

    This site has an extensive listing of pet cemeteries in Canada, England, Singapore, and the United States.

2. www.petcem.com

    This site has something of interest everywhere you click. It belongs to the Hartsdale Pet Cemetery and Crematory in Hartsdale, NY, America's First and Most Prestigious Pet Burial Grounds.

3. http://thunder.prohosting.com/~easyshop/petcem1.html

    Find both pet cemeteries and pet crematoriums listed on this site.

Miscellaneous

1. www.care2.com/channels/solutions/home/14

   This location contains The Five Basics for Nontoxic Cleaning. Be sure to look for The Healthy Pet link while you are visiting this site.

2. www.cgl.uwaterloo.ca/~ssiu/artwork/index.html

   This website has unique and wonderful ferret paintings and excellent photos of ferrets.

3. www.familypetservices.com/toxic_plants.htm

   Check The Family Pet Clinic website for an extensive listing of toxic plants in and around your home.

4. www.ferretcentral.org

   Ferret Central is an invaluable resource whether you are familiar with ferrets or are considering getting one. This site contains training information, ferret organizations and shelters, products, a photo gallery, and more.

5. www.ferret.org

   This is the American Ferret Association, Inc., website. It contains AFA ferret show information and related events, a list of ferret shelters, and vaccination protocols for your ferrets.

6. ferret-request@cunyvm.cuny.edu

   This is not a website but the e-mail address to join the Ferret Mailing List (FML). This is the best resource for ferret-related information including health issues, events, and products. Join the FML to learn about general ferret care and share stories about ferrets.

7. www.marycohen.com/rainbowbridge/rainbowbridge.html

   See a detailed diorama of the Rainbow Bridge, complete with ferrets crossing over.

8. www.modernferret.com

   The website for *Modern Ferret* magazine, the ferret lifestyle magazine, with free newsletter. The magazine contains information on ferret care as well as articles on important health issues. It also has some adorable ferret pictures.

9. www.newrainbowbridge.com

   View the Rainbow Bridge poem as seen here on page 29, as well as ferret products.

10. www.soyouwanna.com/site/syws/ferret/ferret.html

    The So You Wanna Get a Ferret website helps you decide whether a ferret is the right pet for you. It also gives information on choosing your ferret, as well as ferret care and training.

11. www.thepetproject.com/ptff_v2i3.html

    Find a listing of ferret-friendly veterinarians, clubs, shelters, products, and alternative therapies for ferrets here.

12. www.trifl.org/gravy.html

   This is the website for the Triangle Ferret Lovers Ferret Club. Detailed instructions for Bob Church's Chicken Gravy recipes for feeding ferrets and Bob's Insulinoma Series will be found here.

Remembrance Products

1. www.ferretsandfriends.com

   Find a silver angel ferret pin, ferret remembrance teardrop necklace and earrings here, plus other unique and hand-crafted ferret items. You can also find an order form for the jewelry at the end of this book.

2. www.personalcreations.com

   Look for the Sympathy & Memorial link on this website. Be sure to find the Merry Christmas From Heaven Ornament and the My Forever Friend Pet Memorial Frame.

Urns and Markers

1. www.partridge-ent.com/urns.htm

   The Memorial Photo Urn for Pets can be found here, in addition to many other kinds of markers and urns.

2. www.pet-memorial-markers.com

   Vancouver Granite Works in Vancouver, WA, will help you design your own pet memorial marker here.

3. www.theeggcellentcollection.com

   Eggsquisite hand-painted pet memorial egg urns are pictured and sold here. These are truly magnificent.

INDEX

A

Aislyn, 3
Alexander, 5
Almond, 6

B

Baby, 9
Bailey George, 10
Bandit, 11
Bandit, 12
Bandit, 13
Barnaby, 14
Barret, 15
Beans, 17
Bear, 18
Bear, 20
Betty, 21
Bo, 22
Bones, 23
Bones, 24
Booger, 25
BreAnna Lynn, 27
Bubby, 30
Buckwheat, 31
Buddy, 32
Buddy, 33
Buttercup, 34

C

Cael, 36
Caesar, 37
Callie, 38
Cassidy Sioux, 39
Chandler, 40
Cherokee, 41
Chicky, 42
Chomper, 43
Chuck, 44
Chuckie, 45
Clydesdale, 47
Colonel Sanders, 49
Custard, 50

D

Dakota TBear, 51
Dementia Sioux, 53
Diana and Epimetheus, 54

E

Eloise, 55
Ethan, 58

F

Fatboy Slim, 59
Fresno, 60
Furry, 61
Fuzzy, 62

G

Godiva, 63
Gonzo, 64
Gypsy, 65

H

Handsome, 66
Heidi, 67
Hermes, 68
Houdini, 70
Hubert, 71
Humphrey, 72

J

JB, 73
Jasmine, 74
Jasmine, 76
Jasmine, 77
Jasper, 78
Jasper, 80
Jeremy, 81
Jesse, 83
Jewel, 86
Junior, 87

K

Kari, 88
Kasper, 89
Katie, 90
Kirby, 91
Koala, 93
Kuma, 94
Kyle, 95

L

Little Fang, 96
Littleone, 100
Love, 101
Lucky, 102
Lucky, 104

M

Major Burns, 105
Mandrake, 106
Maxie, 108
Maximilian, 109
Meep, 110
Miss Kitty, 111
Mistie Sioux, 112
Mocha, 113
Monkey, 114
Mr. Edward, 117
Mr. Noble Man, 120
Mr. Peabody, 121
Murray, 122

N

Nipper, 123

O

Odie, 124
Oldguy, 125
Opie, 126

P

PB, 127
Paladin, 129
Pato, 130
Peanut, 131
Peedee, 132
PePe, 133
Pjatten, 134
Pogo, 135
Popcorn, 136
Pugsley, 138

Q

Quasimoto, 139

R

Rascal, 141
Rebecca Sioux, 142
Renate, 146
Renny, 147
Rocky, 148
Rocky, 149
Romeo, 150
Rusty, 151
Rusty, 152

S

Sammy, 153
Samson, 154
Sandie, 155
Sassy, 156
Simba, 157
Skyler, 158
Snowy, 160
Sonny, 161
Sonny, 163
Sophie, 164
Squeeky and Snowball, 165
Stevie, 166
Stinky, 169
Surabi, 170
Sweet Amadeus Van Gogh, 171
Sweetie, 173

T

Tasha, 176
Tasha, 177
Tassie, 178
Tawnee Sioux, 179
Thelma, 181
Tia, 183
Tiny, 184
Tootles, 185
Tucker, 186
Tucker, 188
Tyson, 189

W

Wanda, 191
Warlock, 192
Whiskey Sour, 195
White Russian, 196
White Russian, 197
Winnie, 198
Wolf, 199

Z

Zeus, 201
Zeus, 202
Ziggy, 203
Ziggy, 204
Zorro, 205
Zuzu, 206

FERRET REMEMBRANCE JEWELRY ORDER FORM

To order remembrance jewelry, make copies of this page and mail to the address listed below. Send payment of $32.85 for one jewelry item (price includes shipping). Add $29.00 for each additional item. Jewelry is rushed to you by USPS Priority Mail.

Silver Angel Ferret Pin   Silver Teardrop Earrings   Silver Teardrop Necklace

Number of Silver Angel Ferret Pins:	_____
Number of Ferret Remembrance Teardrop Necklaces:	_____
Number of Ferret Remembrance Teardrop Earring Sets: (the earrings also make great tie tacks, collar and lapel pins)	_____
Amount Enclosed: $	
Name:	
Street Address:	
City, State, Zip:	
E-mail Address:	

Make check or money order payable and send to:

        Donna Austin
        9493 Dutch Hollow Road
        Rixeyville, VA 22737

 Use your credit card on the Internet at PayPal.com and make payable to FuzzbeanCrossing@aol.com.

ALL PROCEEDS USED TO CARE FOR RESCUED FERRETS

FERRET PRINT SELECTIONS

#1

#2

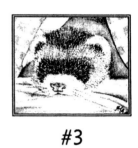
#3

(Print #1 is in full color)

#4

#5

#6

#7

#8

FERRET PRINTS ORDER FORM

To order ferret art prints, make copies of this page and mail to the address listed below. Send payment of $11.85 for each 5"x7" print and $13.85 for each 8"x10" print (price includes shipping). Save on shipping charges by ordering additional prints. For each additional print, add $8.00 (5"x7") or $10.00 (8"x10"). All prints are rushed to you by USPS Priority Mail.

Please print legibly:

Print Numbers (found under each print on the previous page):
Indicate the quantity next to each print number (example: #3-2 ea.)
Amount Enclosed: $
Name:
Street Address:
City, State, Zip:
E-mail Address:

Make check or money order payable and send to:

> Donna Austin
> 9493 Dutch Hollow Road
> Rixeyville, VA 22737

 Use your credit card on the Internet at PayPal.com and make payable to FuzzbeanCrossing@aol.com.

ALL PROCEEDS USED TO CARE FOR RESCUED FERRETS

BOOK MAIL ORDER FORM

To order additional copies of *Fuzzbean Crossing*, make copies of this page and mail to the address listed below. Send payment of $19.80 for each book (price includes shipping). All books are rushed to you by USPS Priority Mail.

Please print legibly:

No. of Copies:	Amount Enclosed: $
Name:	
Street Address:	
City, State, Zip:	
E-mail Address:	

Make check or money order payable and send to:

>Donna Austin
>9493 Dutch Hollow Road
>Rixeyville, VA 22737

 Use your credit card on the Internet at PayPal.com and make payable to FuzzbeanCrossing@aol.com.

ALL PROCEEDS USED TO CARE FOR RESCUED FERRETS

Donna Austin has dedicated her life to her passion, which is caring for rescued ferrets since 1992. In addition to sixteen ferrets, she is caretaker to Paulie and Freckles, two domestic long-hair cats. With a background as a computer instructor for many years, she has also conducted educational seminars on ferrets in schools, pet stores and at SPCA events, and never misses an opportunity to talk to people about ferret care and behavior. Her website, www.ferretsandfriends.com, has products for people who love ferrets, as well as healthy food and supplies for dogs and cats. There is a product line on the website consisting of note cards, prints suitable for framing, T-shirts, mouse pads, and tote bags, using the beautiful illustrations in this book. She has designed custom ferret jewelry, cookie cutters and other unique items.

As author of several software training manuals, Ms. Austin resides 75 miles west of Washington, DC, in the beautiful Virginia countryside.

&

Illustrator Marta Chidester Mitchell lives with her husband Bert and their family in southern Utah, where she teaches art in the public schools. Mitchell is a well-known artist in her community and has had her work exhibited and published on numerous occasions. She and her husband run a business selling ferret T-shirts, greeting cards and other personalized ferret-related products. For additional information on her artwork or ferret products, write to Marta at ferret-lady@miners-peak.com.

&

Poet Liz Blackburn lives in Montrose, Colorado, where she is a substitute teacher, a mom and the wife of a working cowboy. She graduated from the University of North Dakota in 1969 and settled in the Colorado mountains to fulfill her dreams of country living and to spend as much time as possible on horseback. Her passion in life has always been her love of animals and her deep love for Little Fang, her first and only ferret, who is the soul of her poetry.